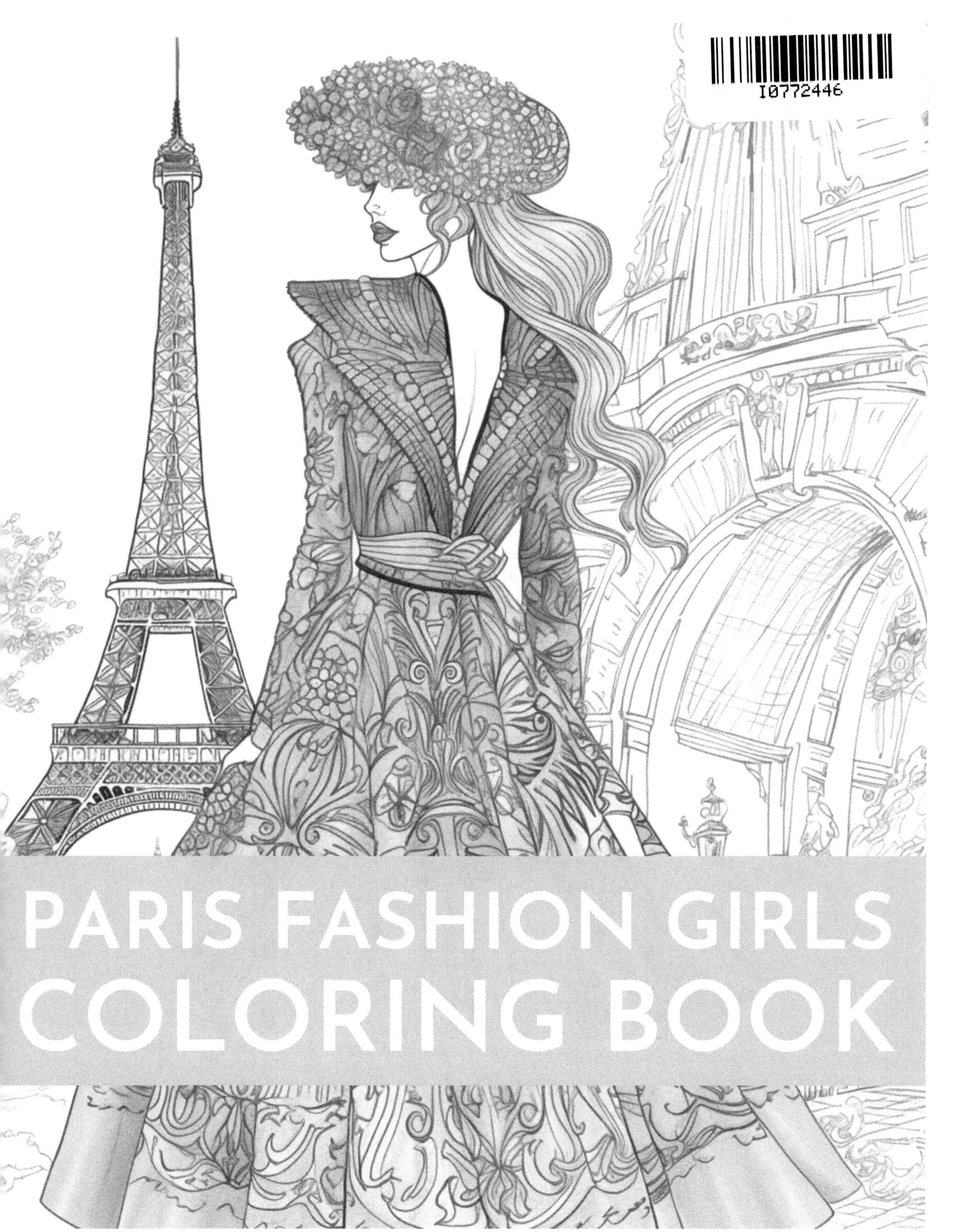

I0772446
PARIS FASHION GIRLS
COLORING BOOK

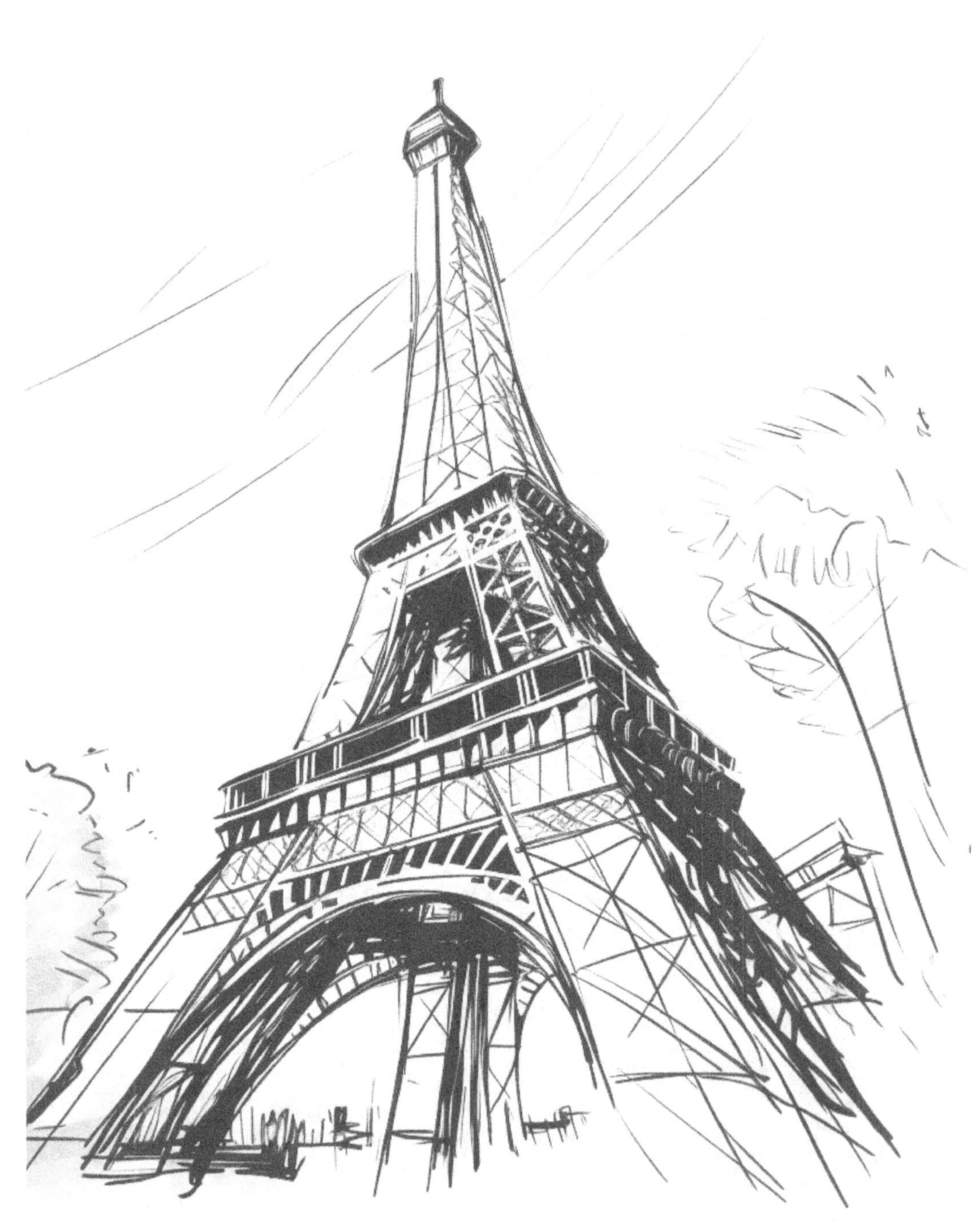

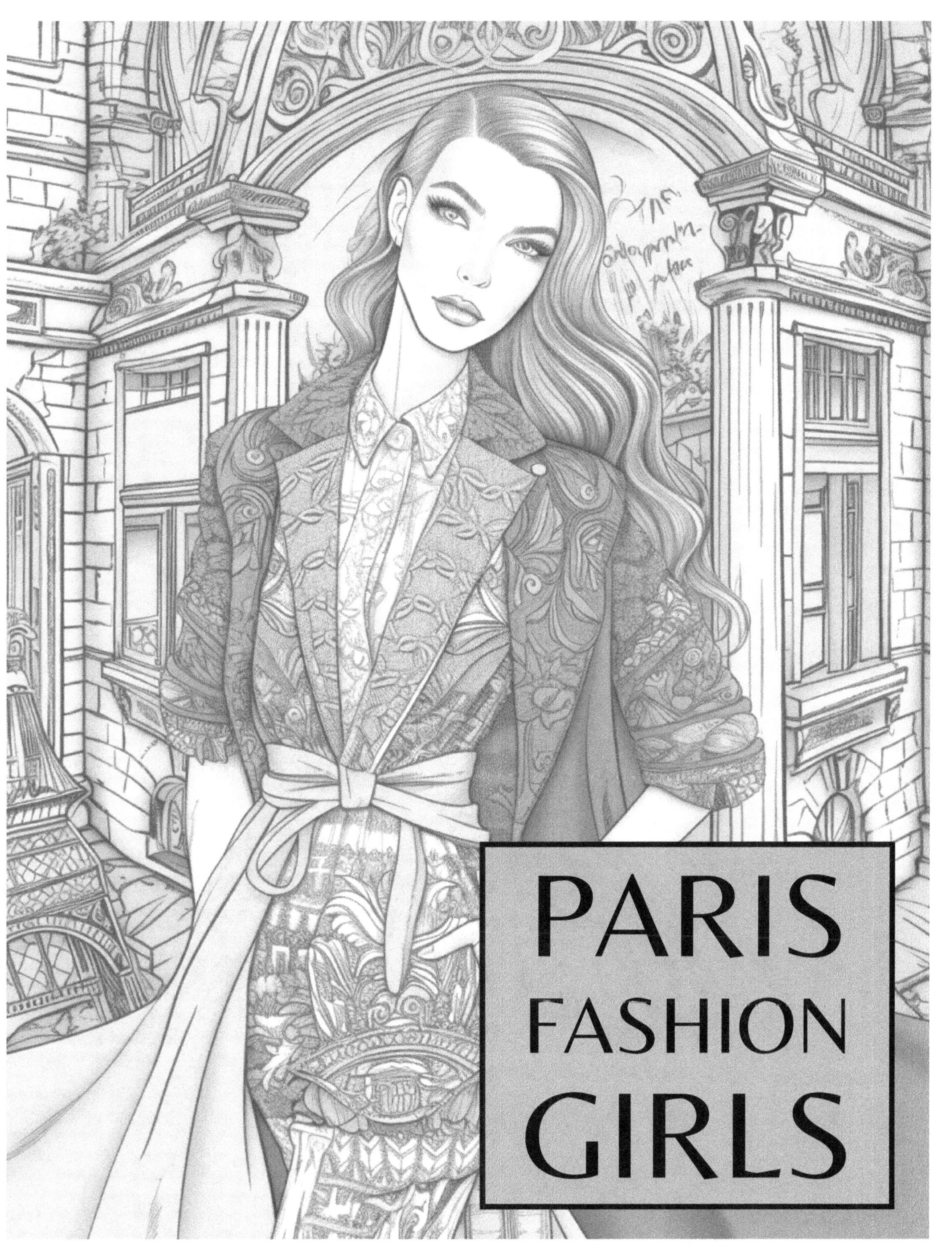

PARIS
FASHION
GIRLS

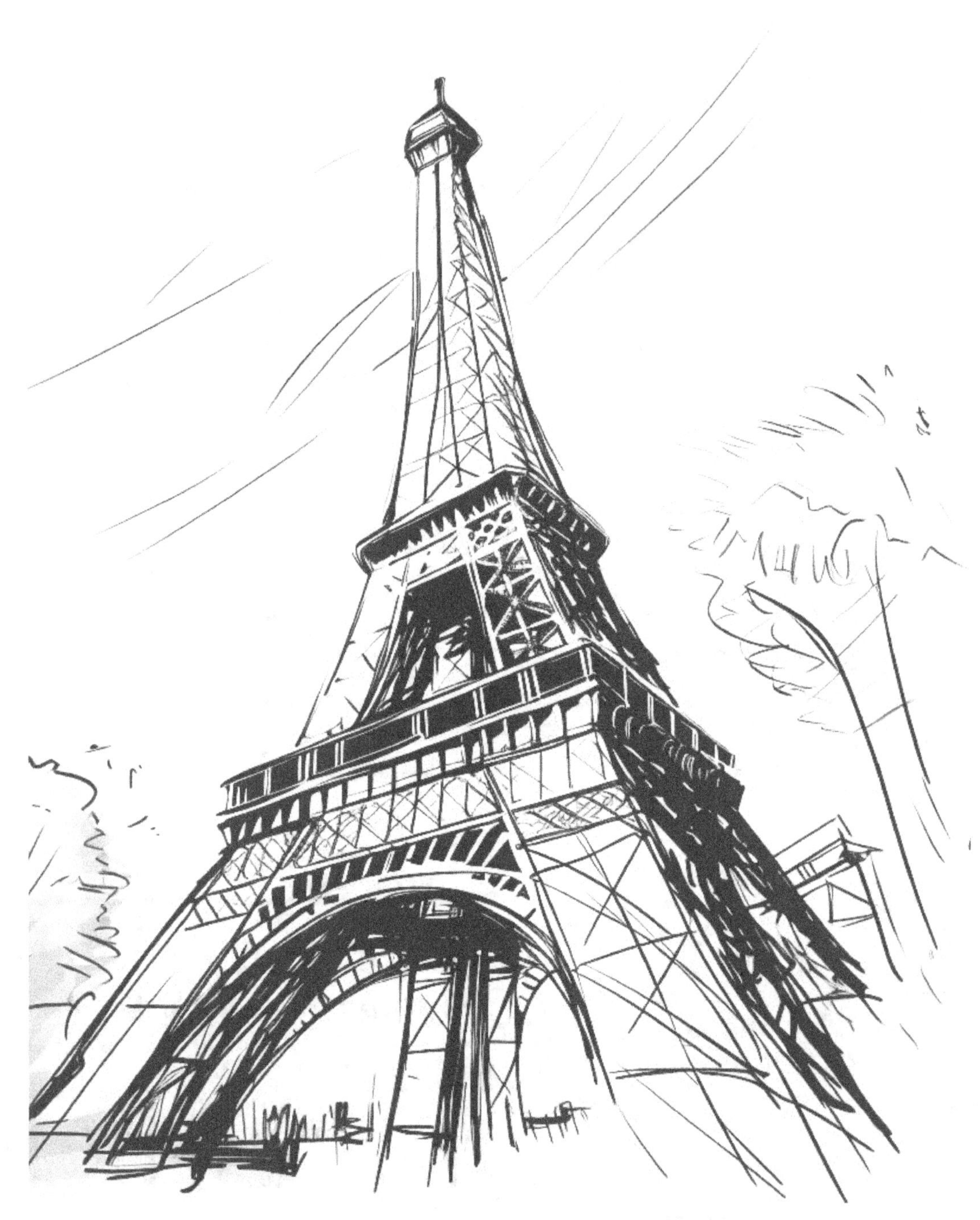

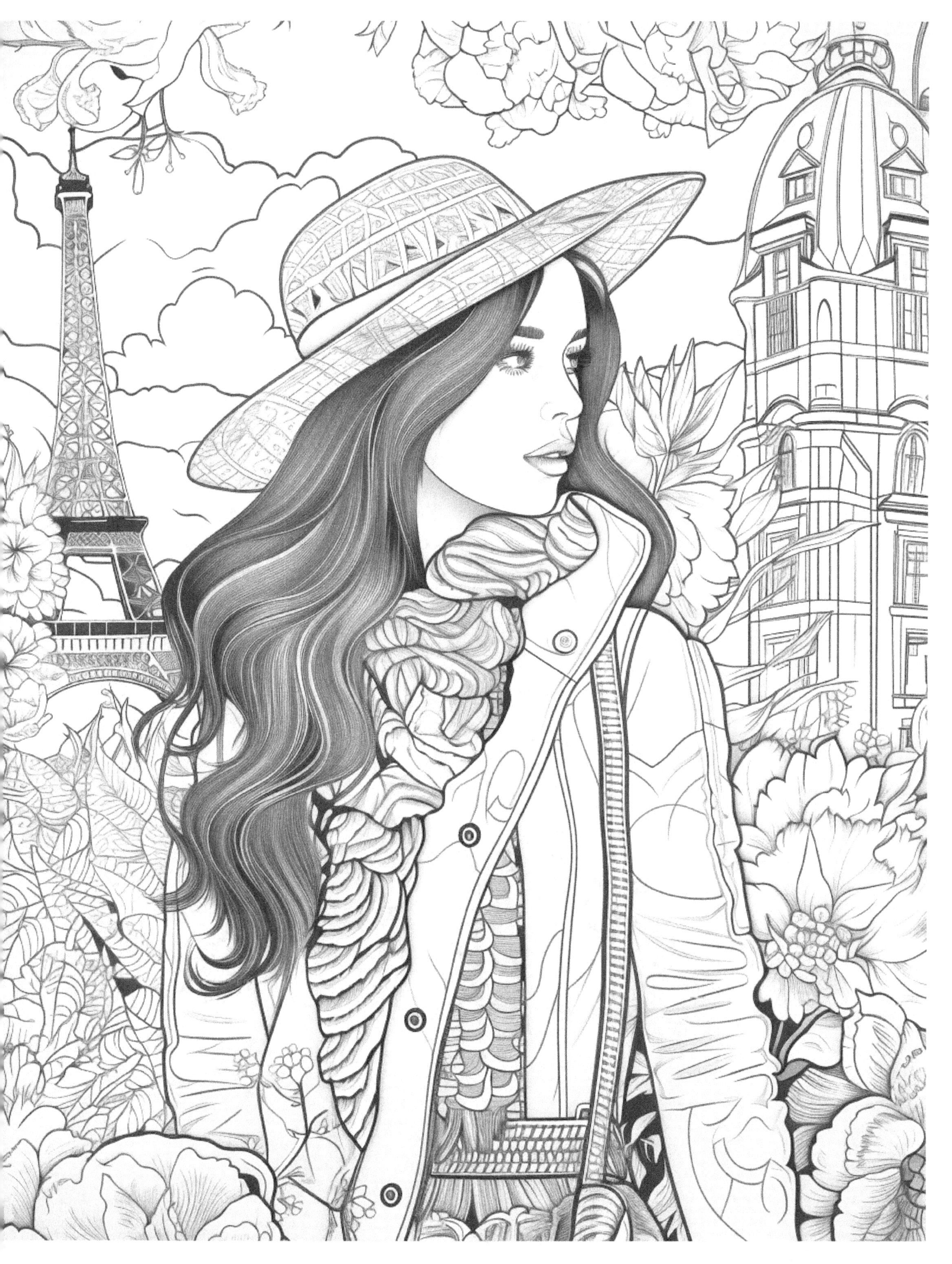

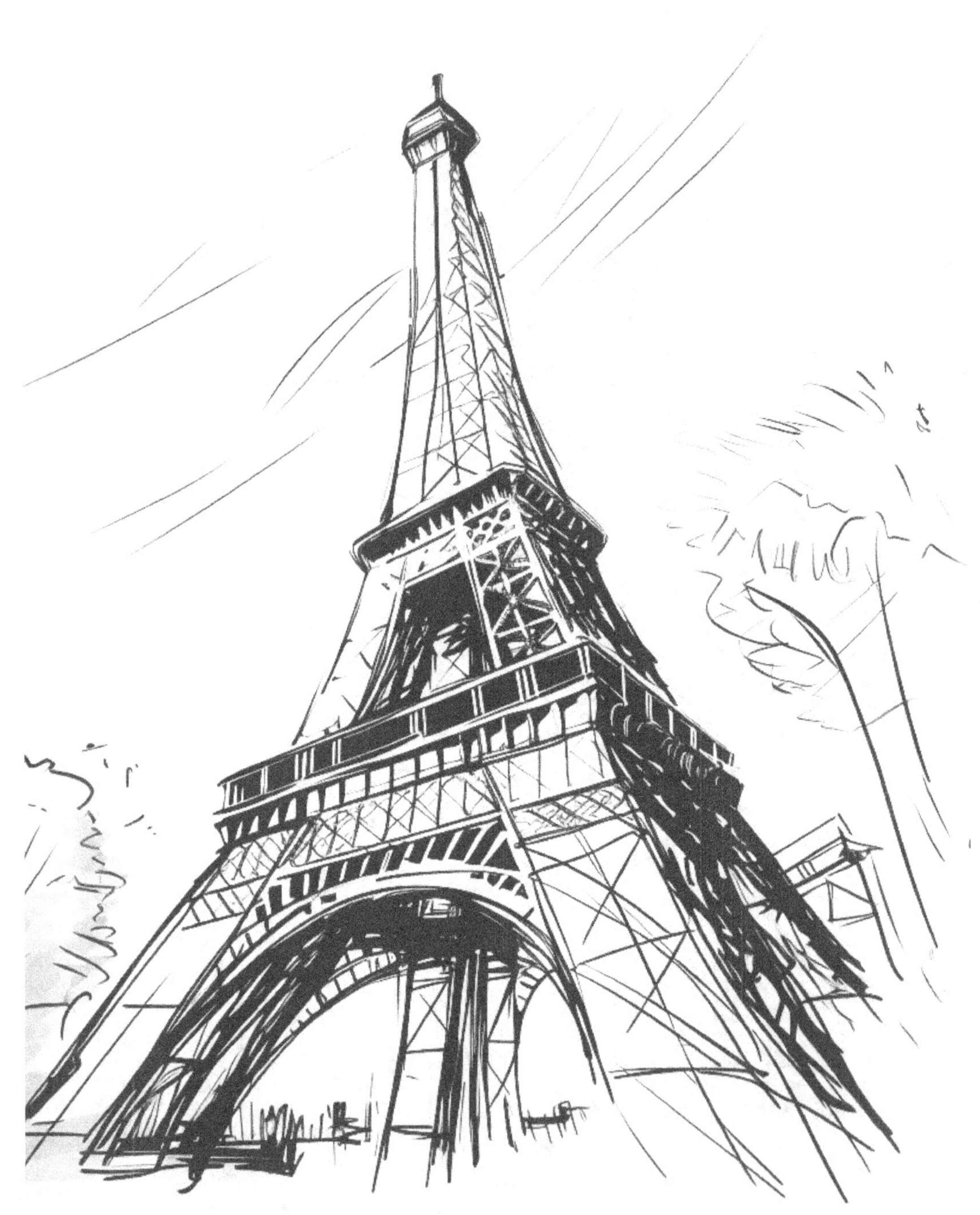

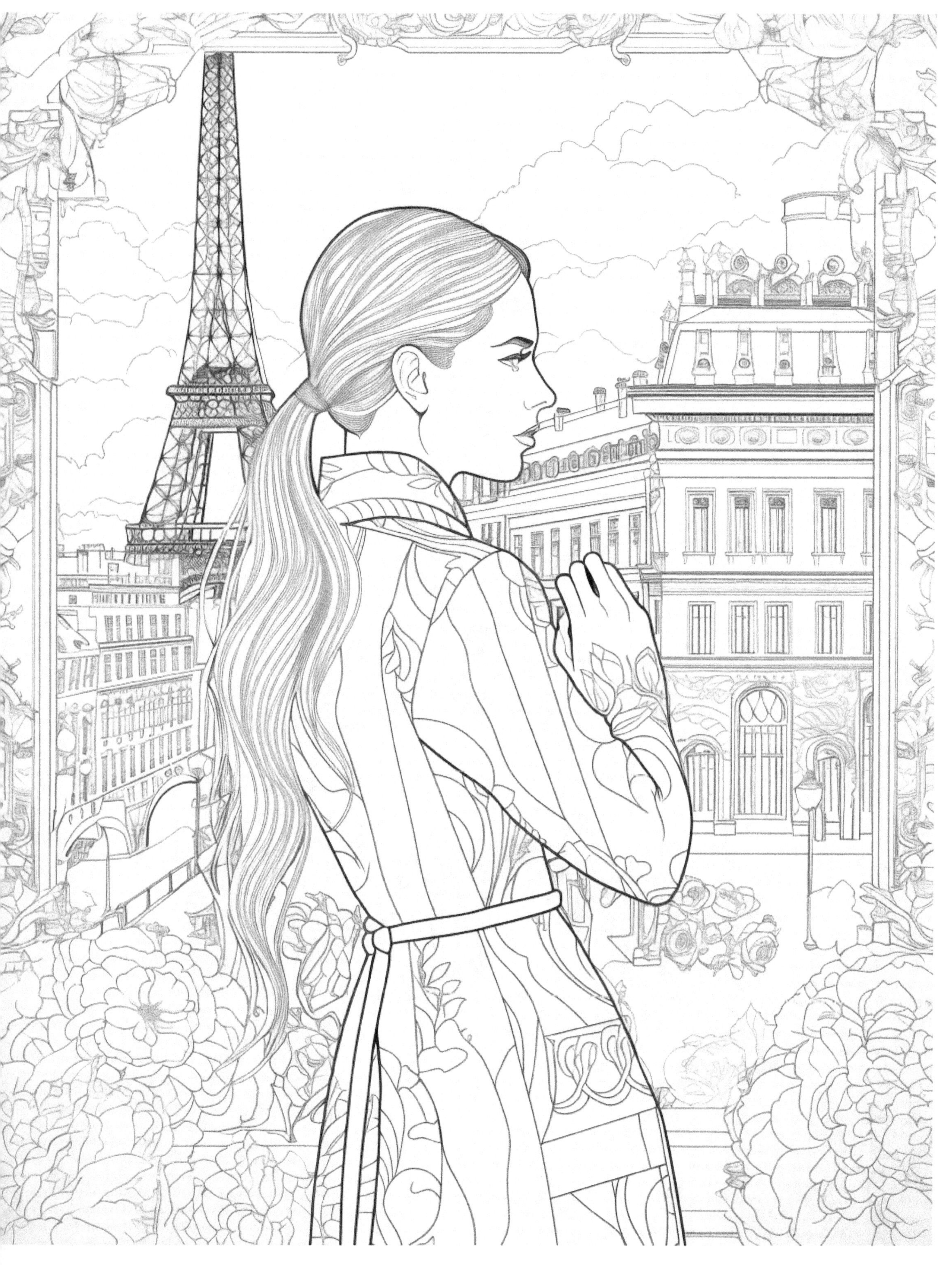

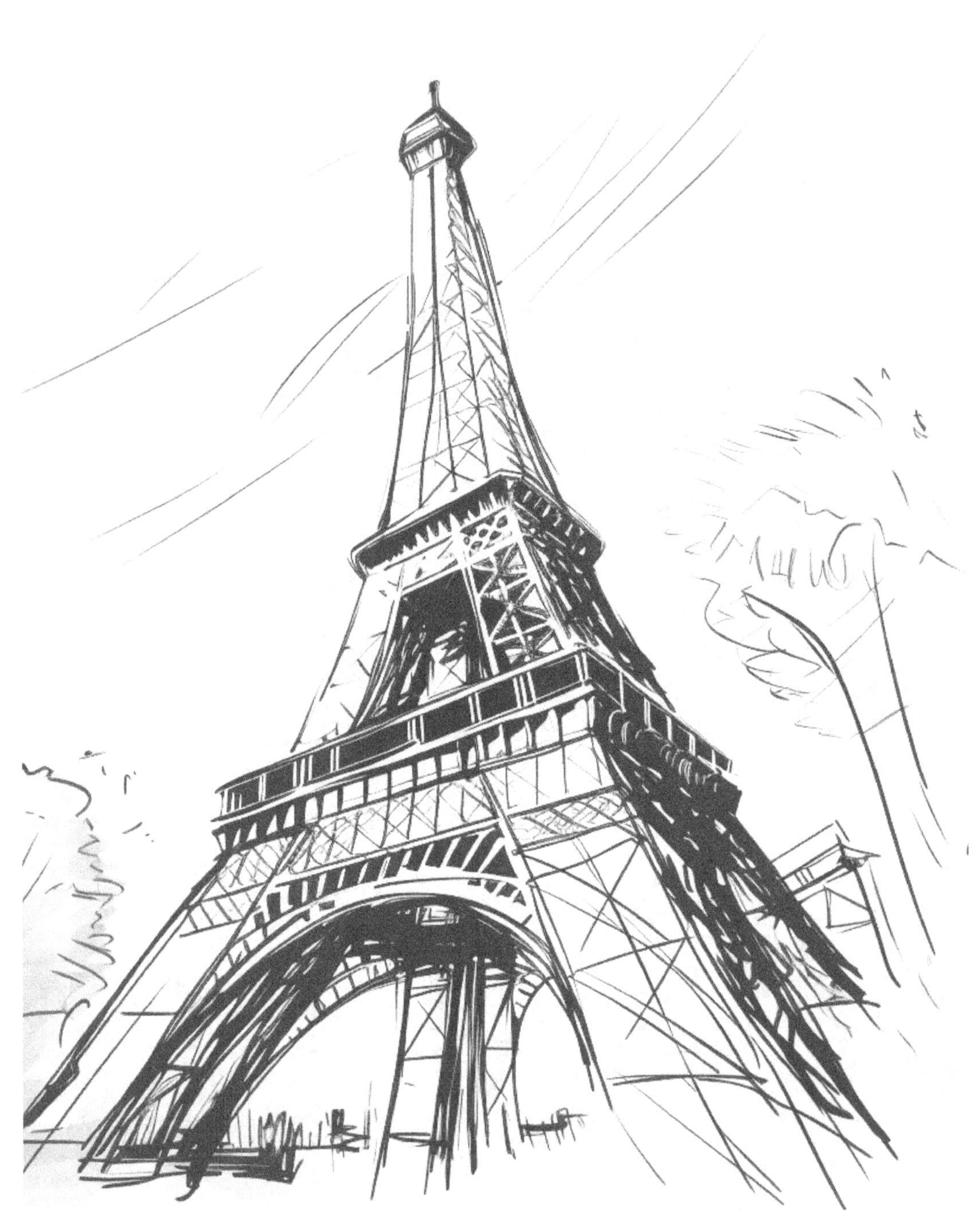

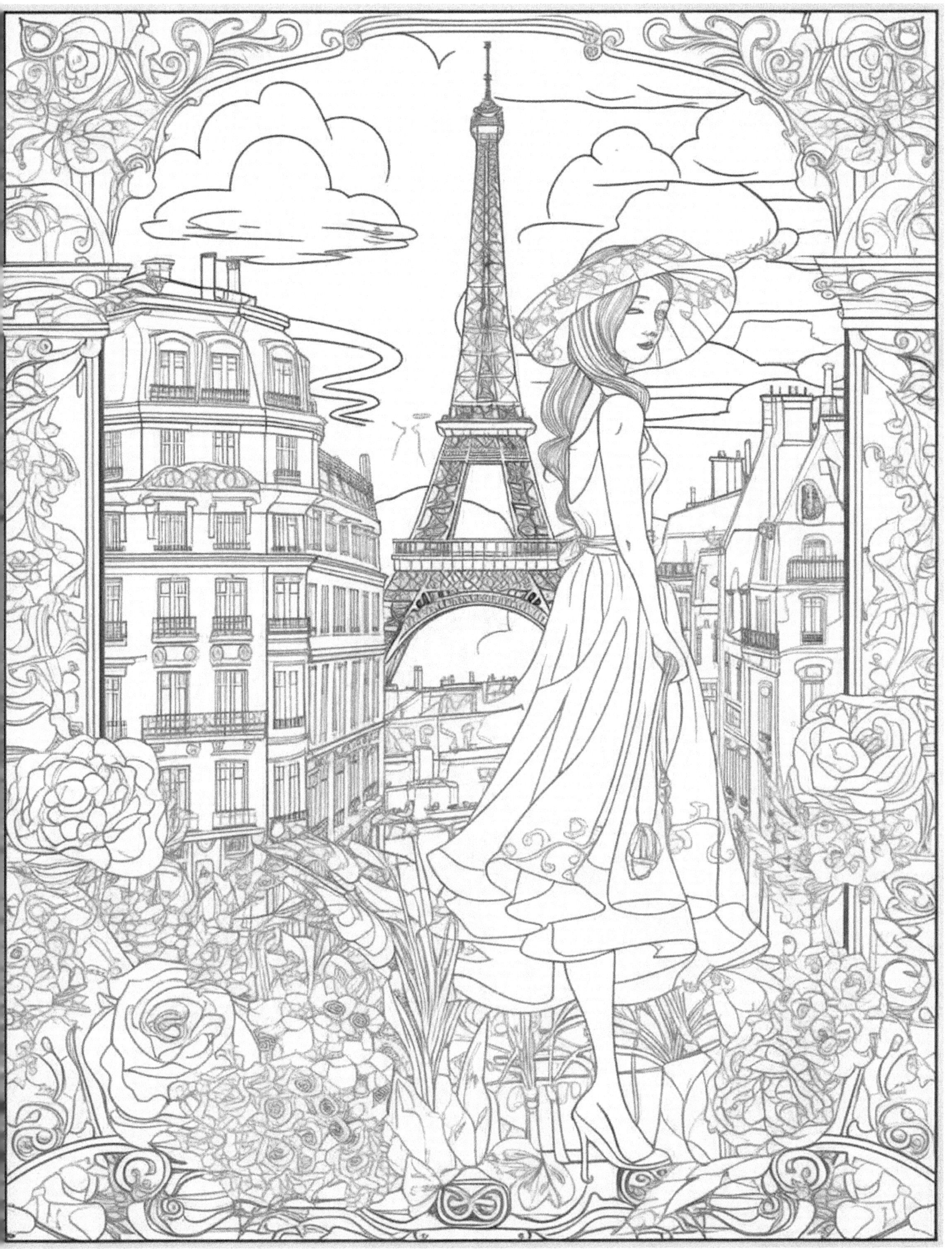

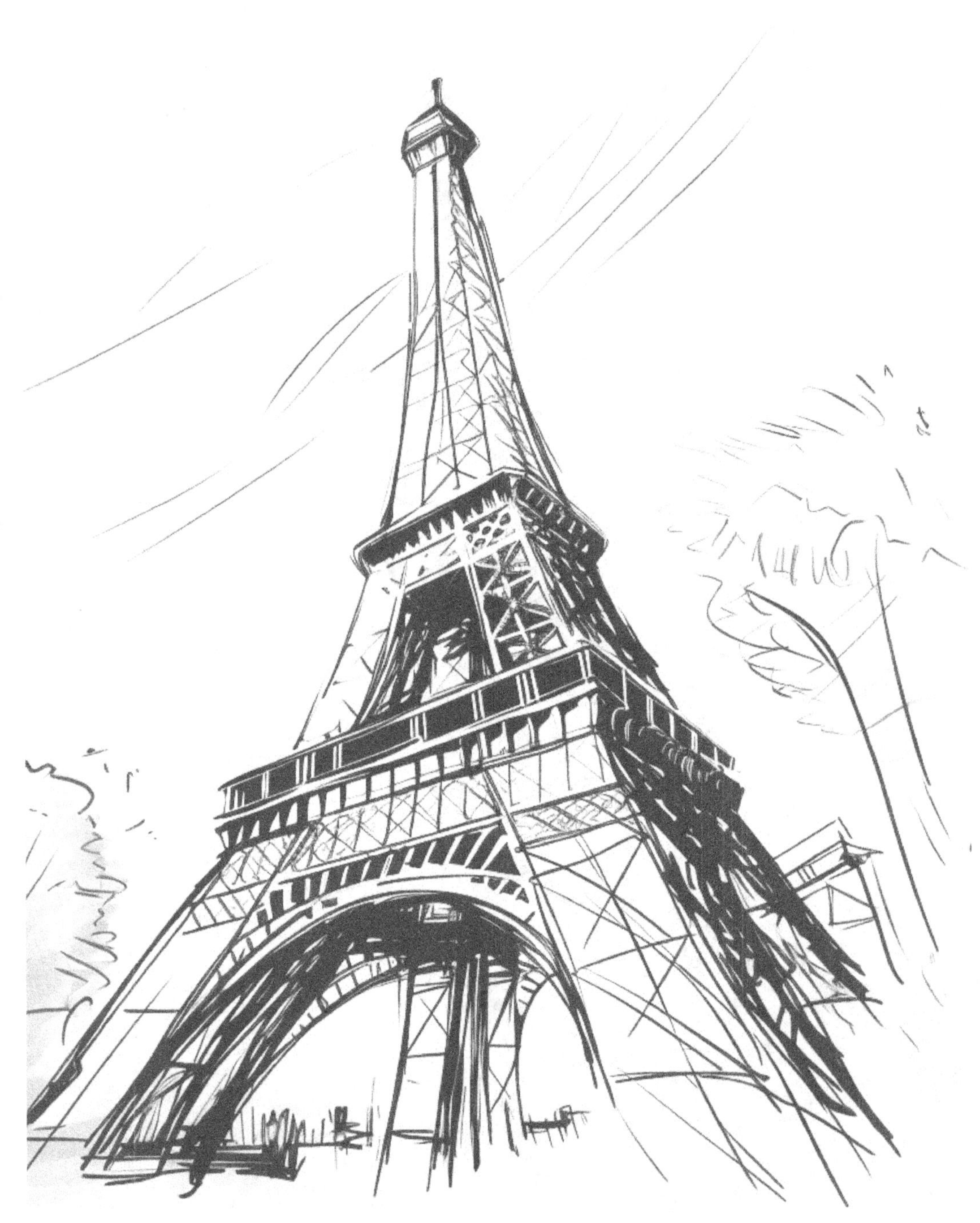

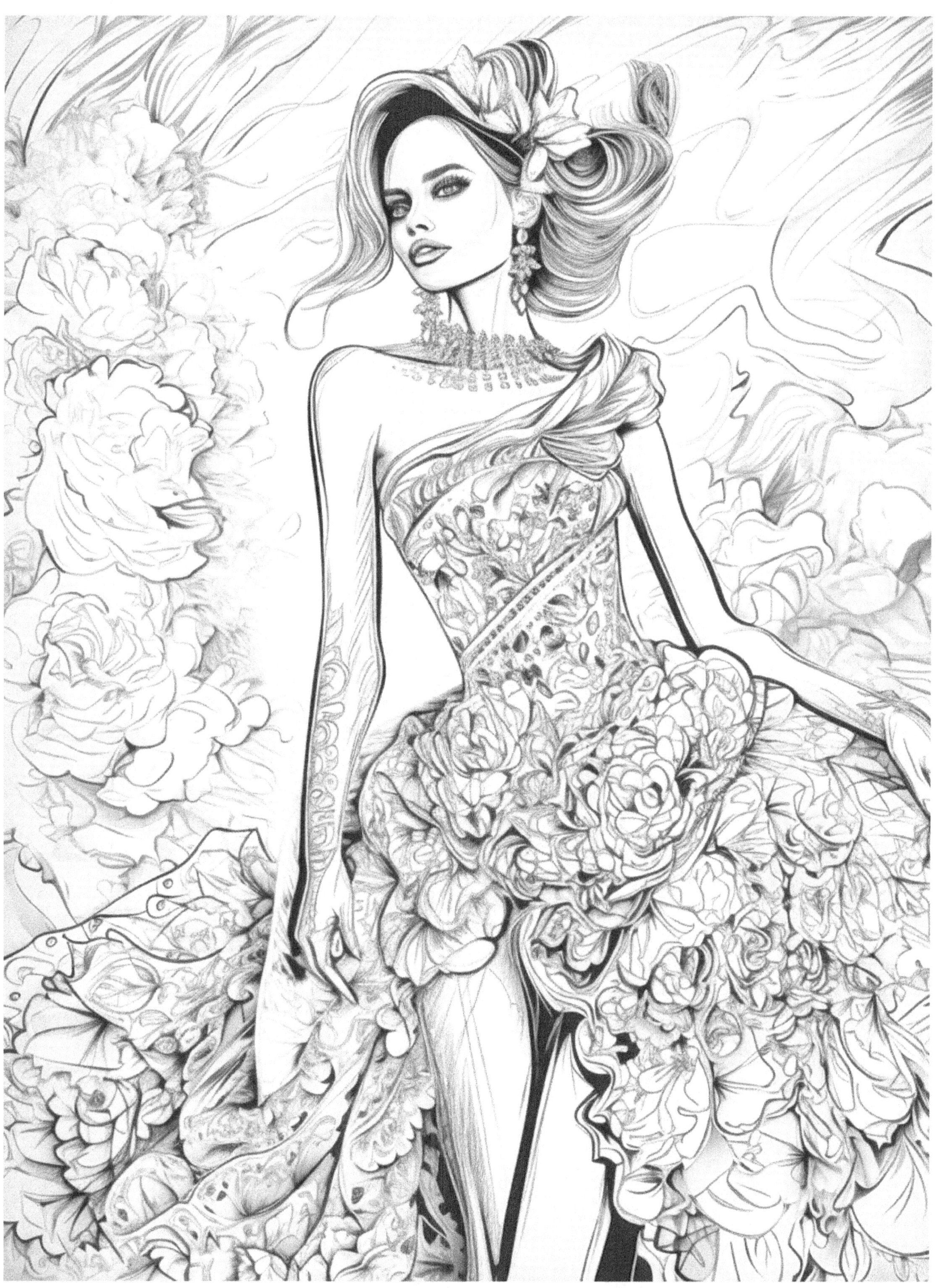

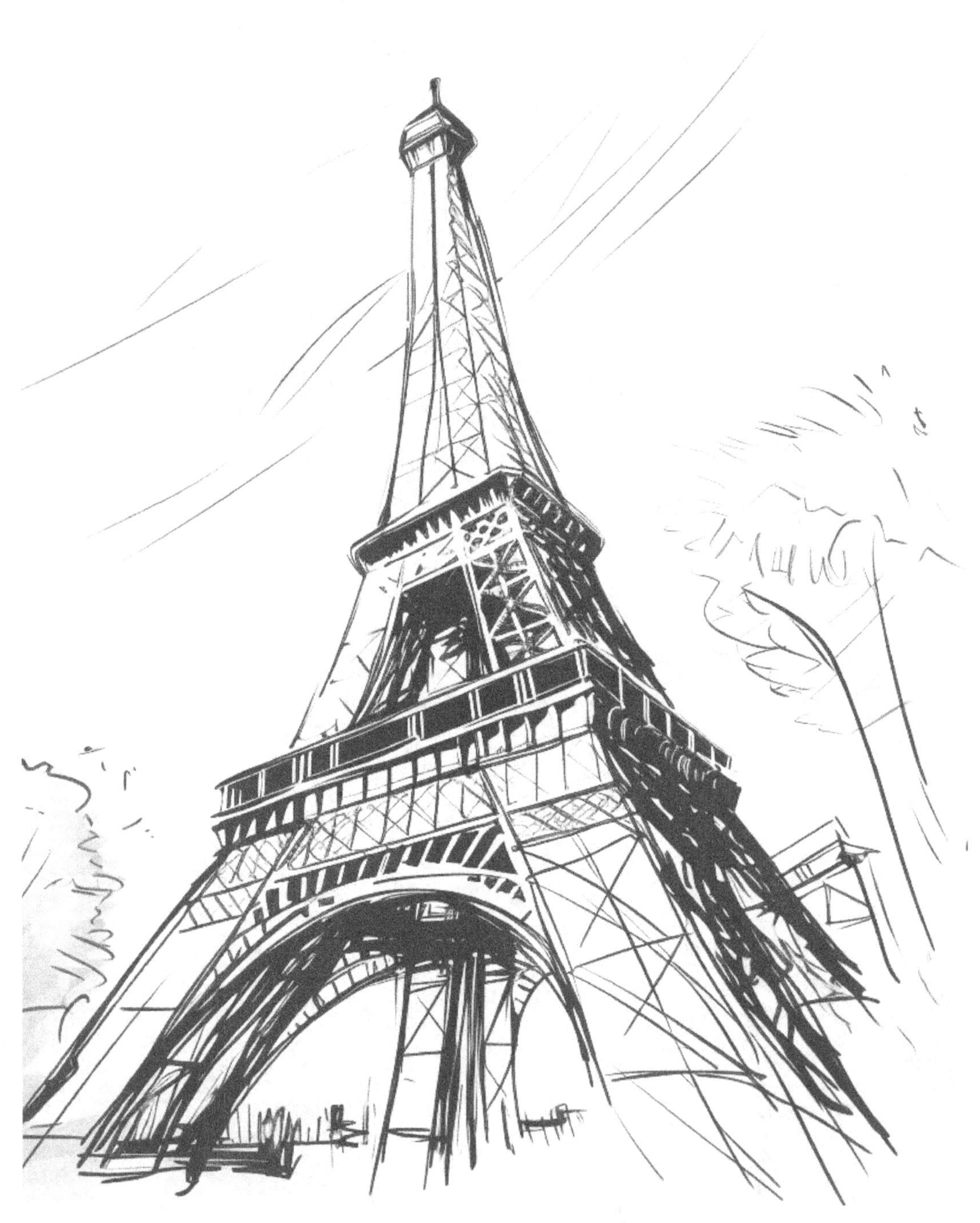

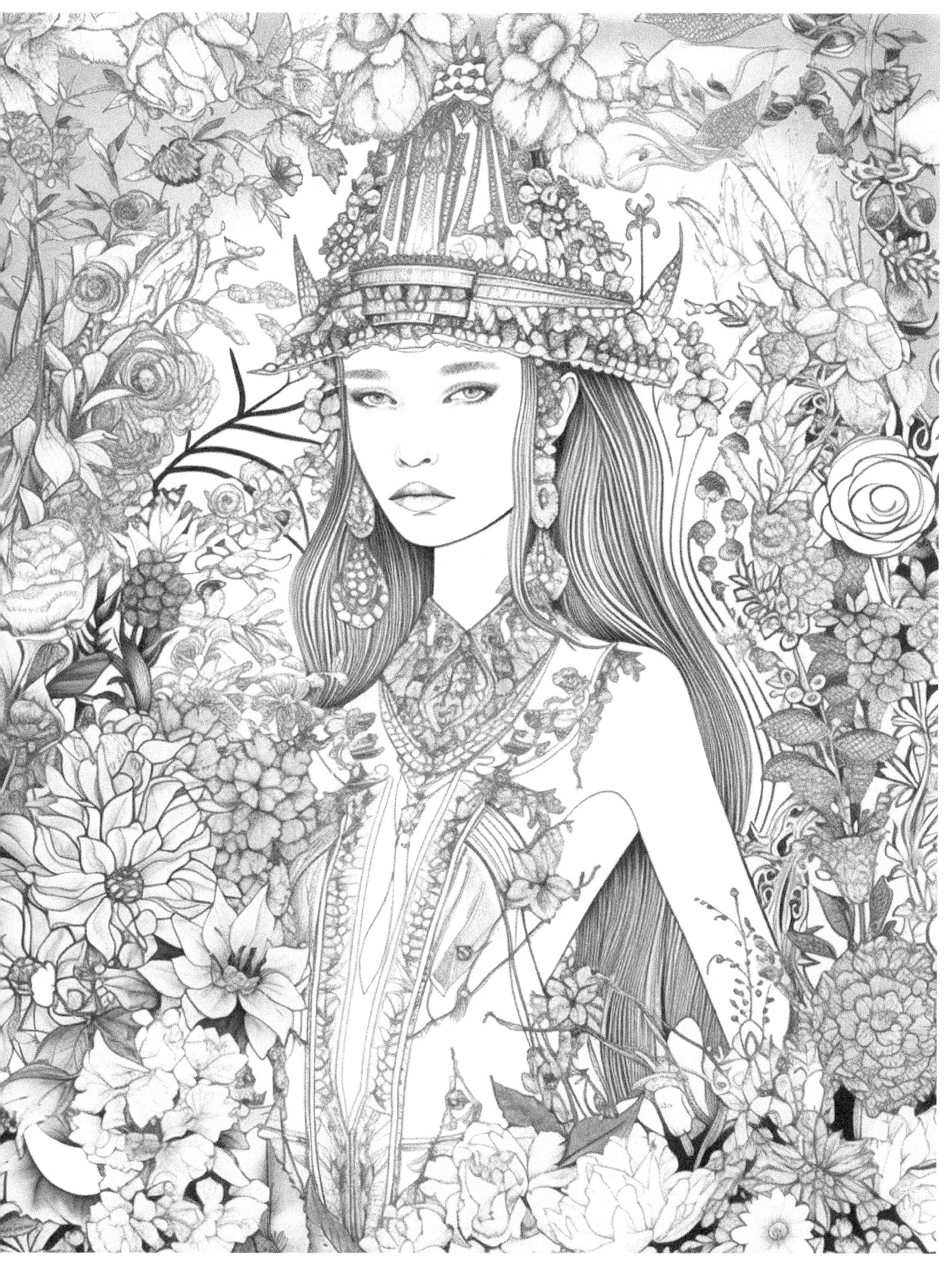

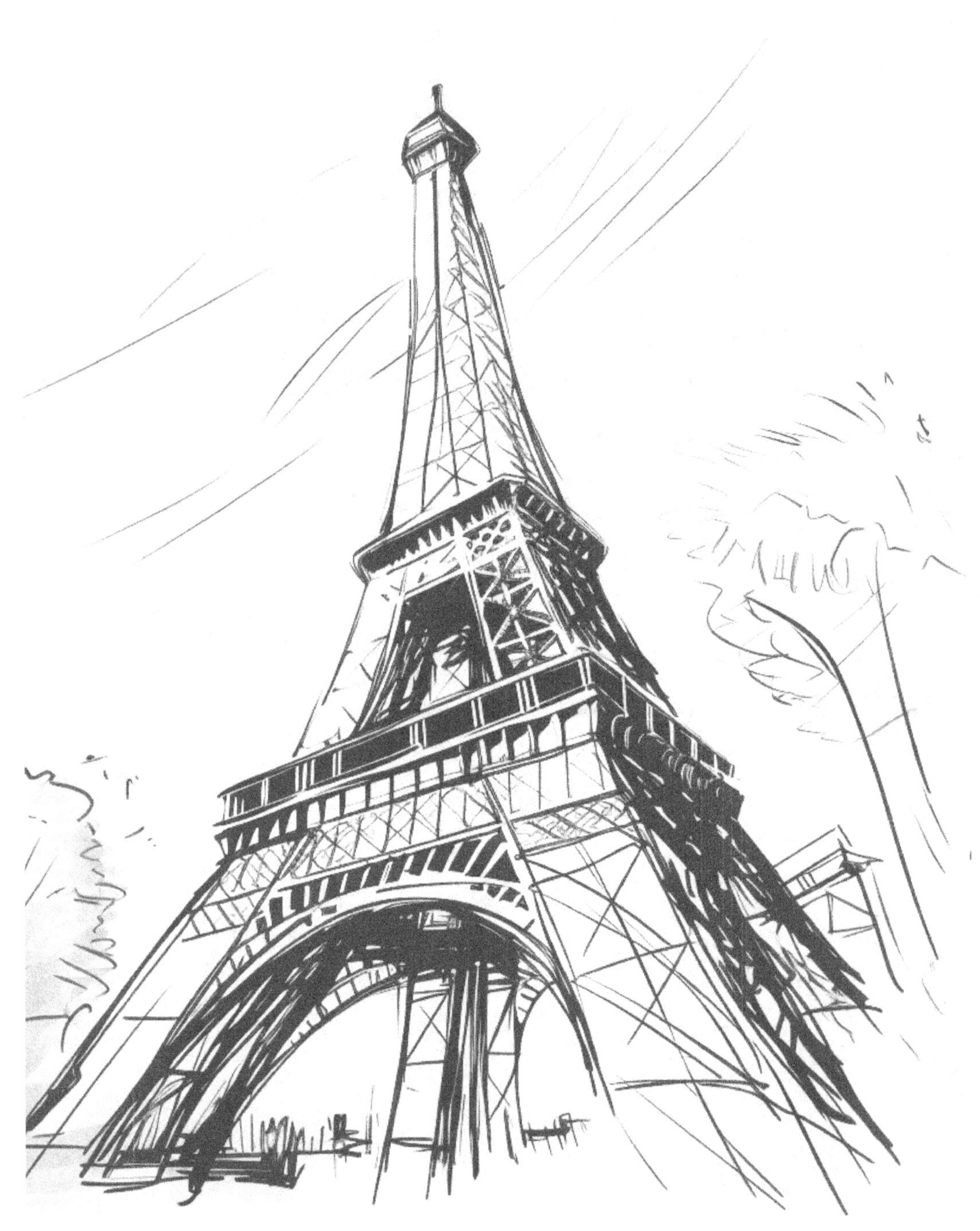

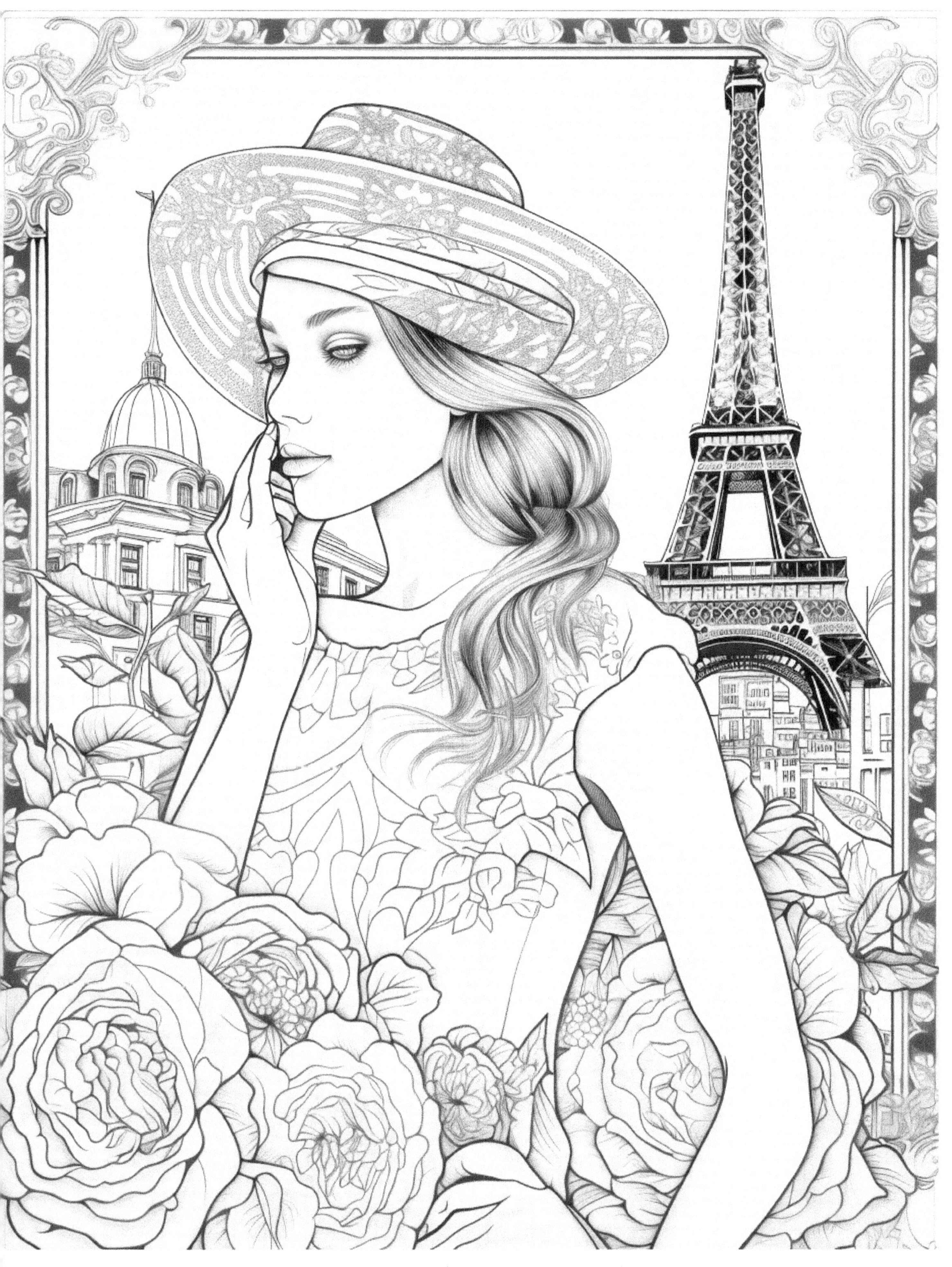

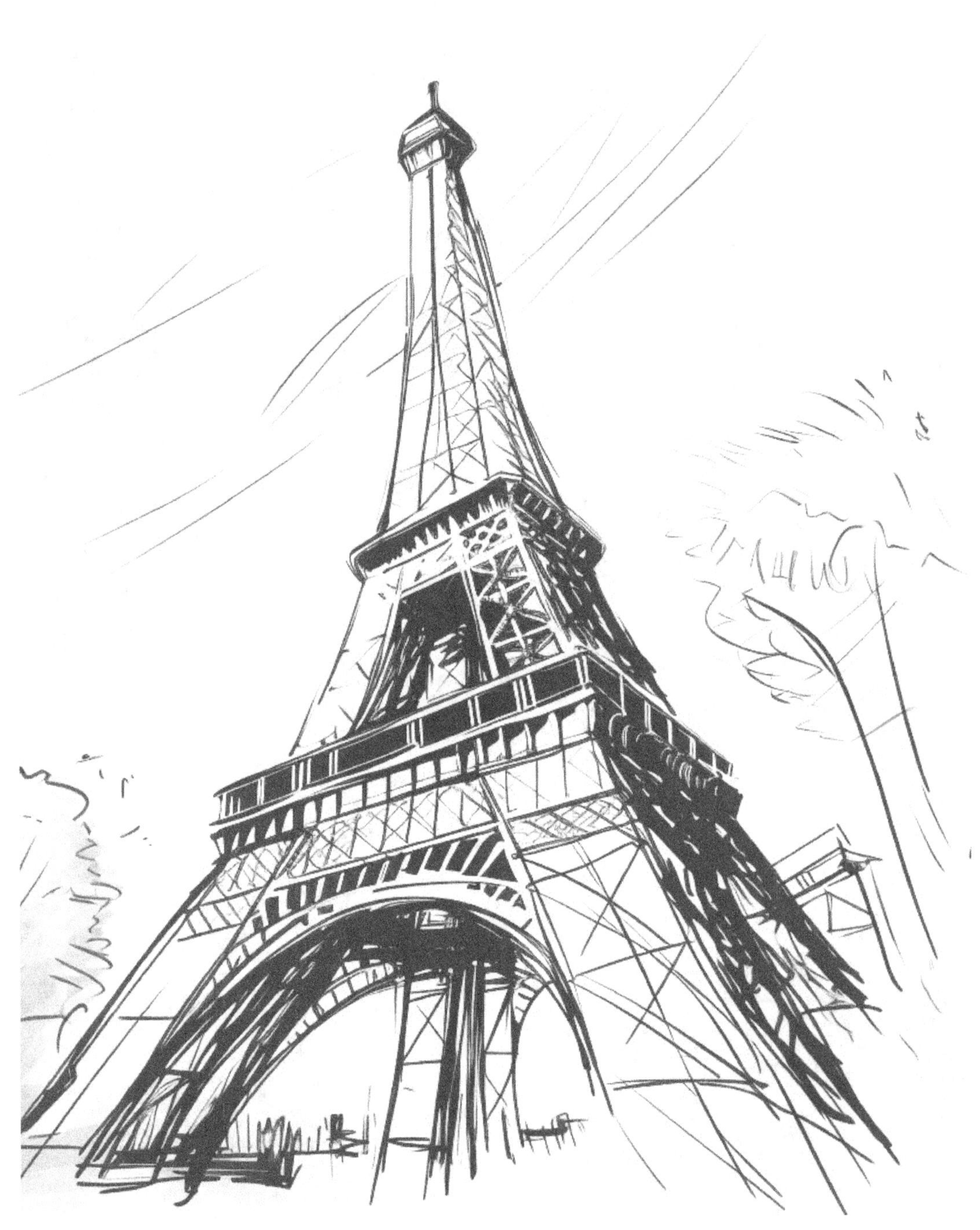

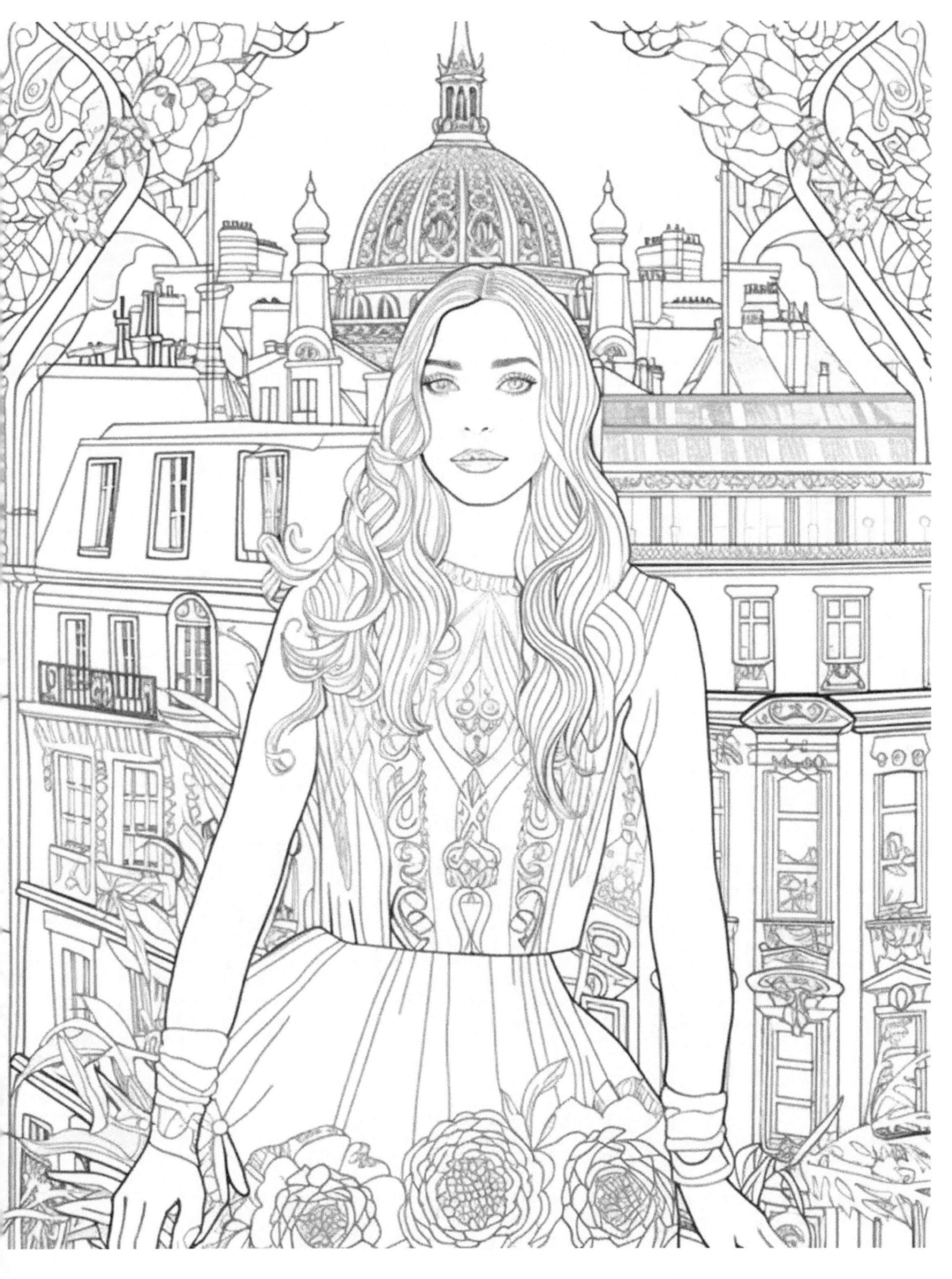

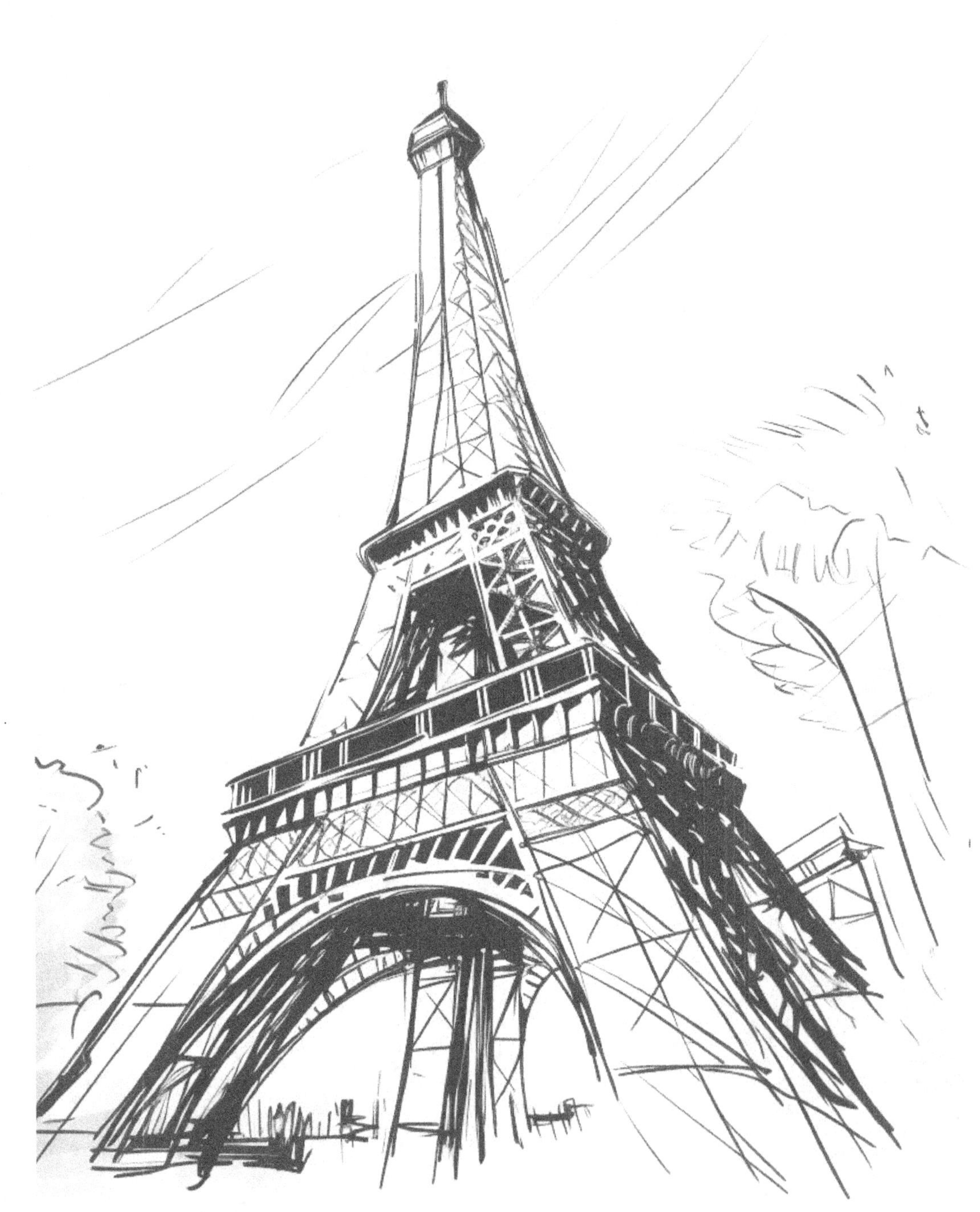

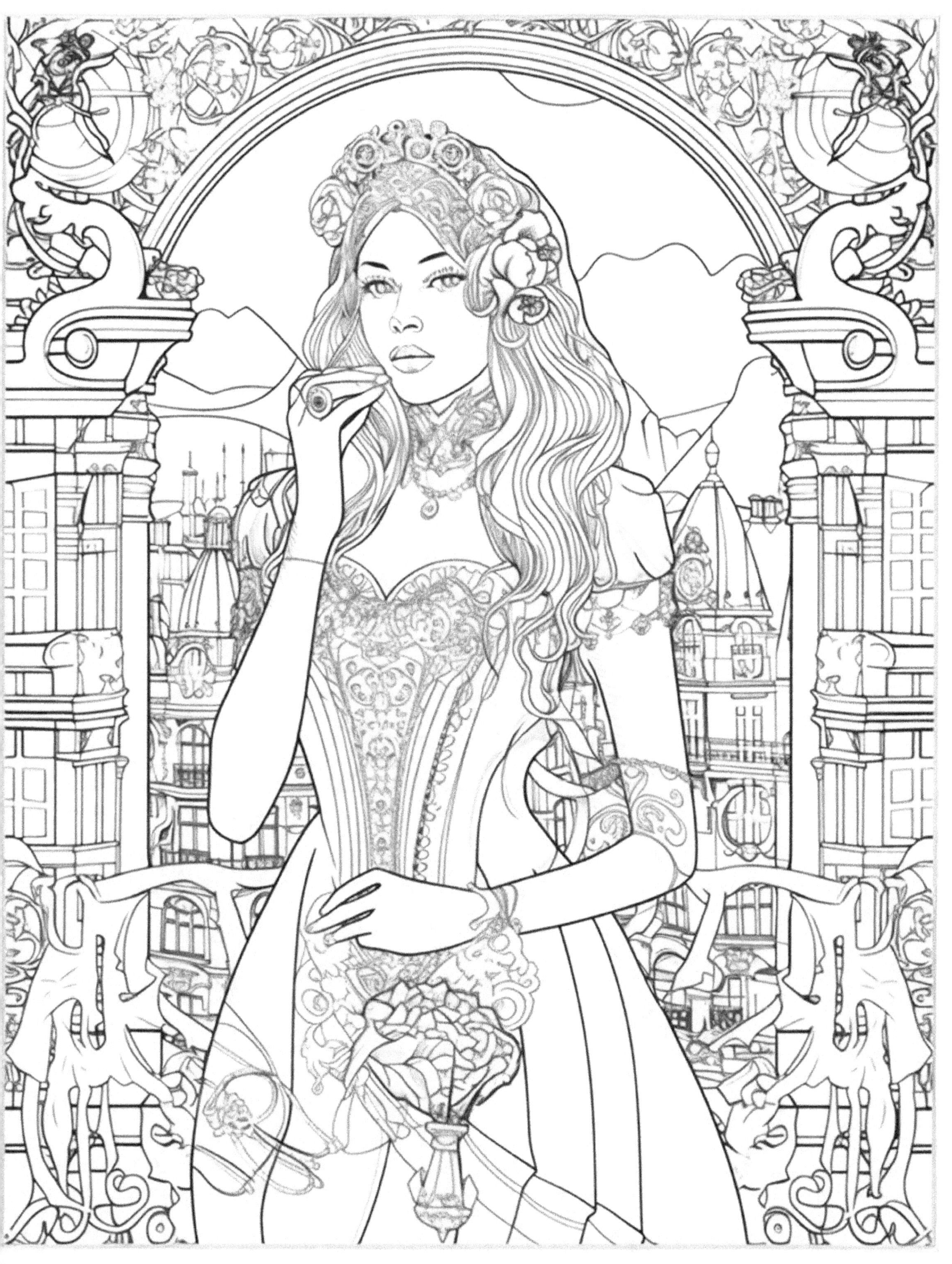

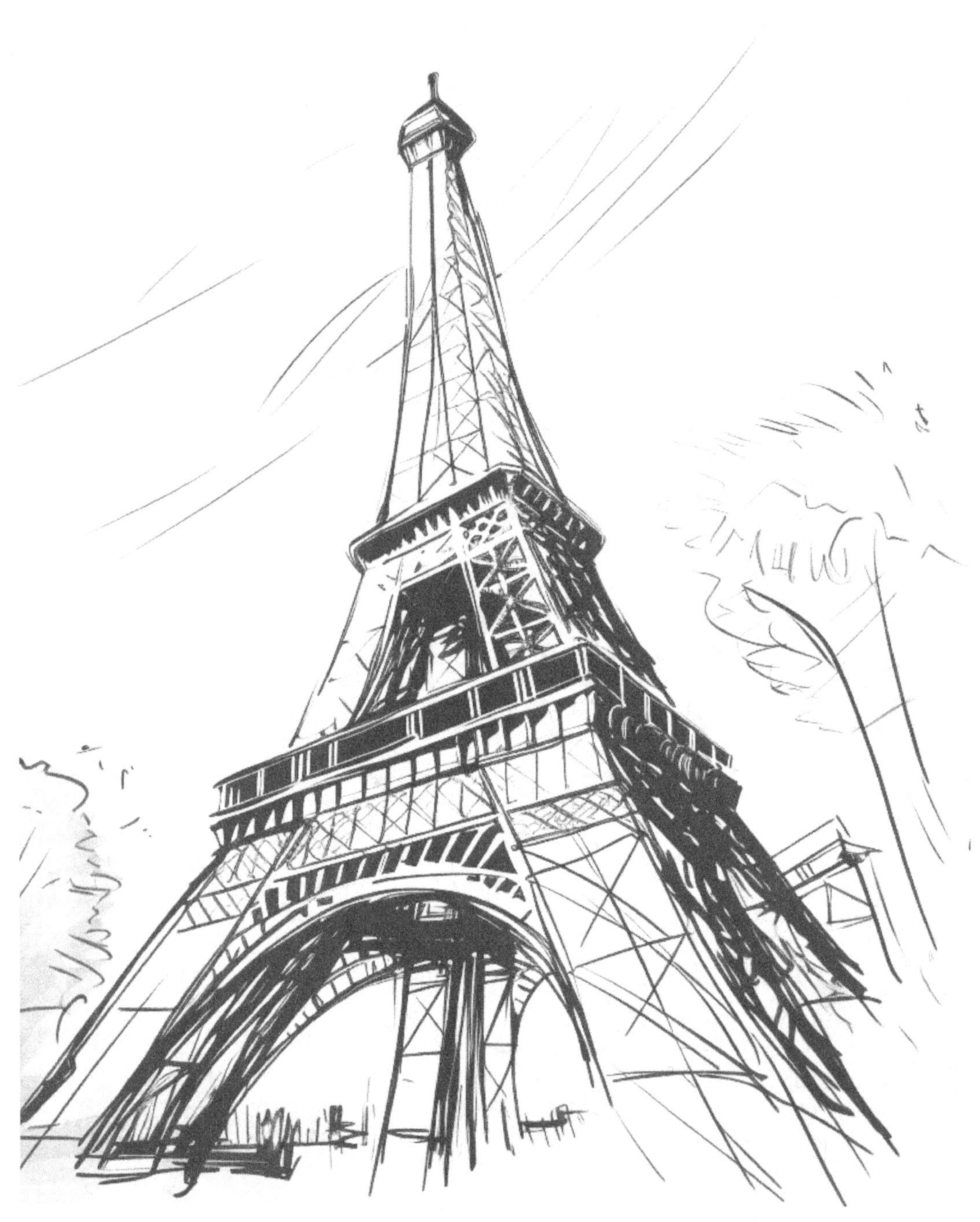

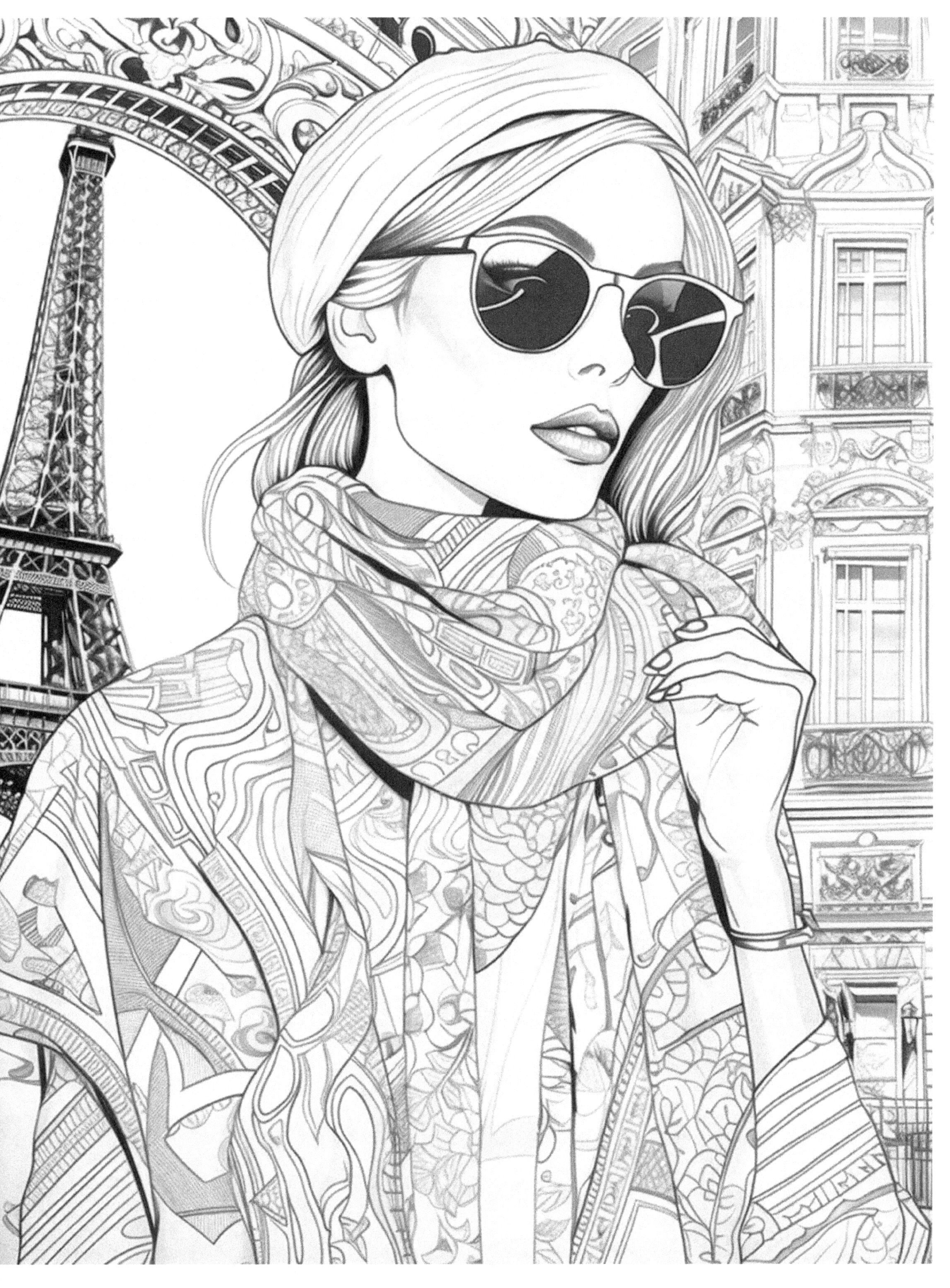

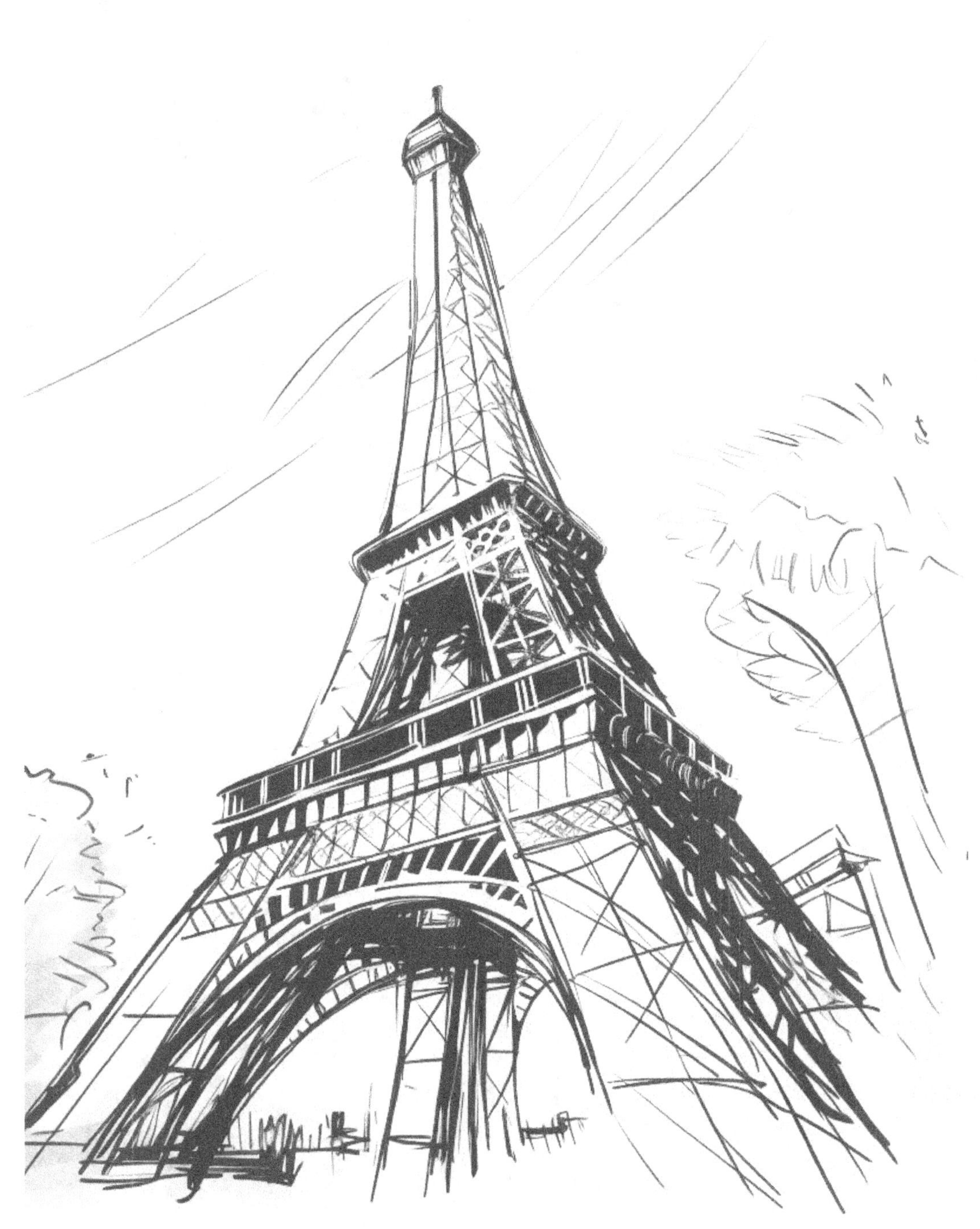

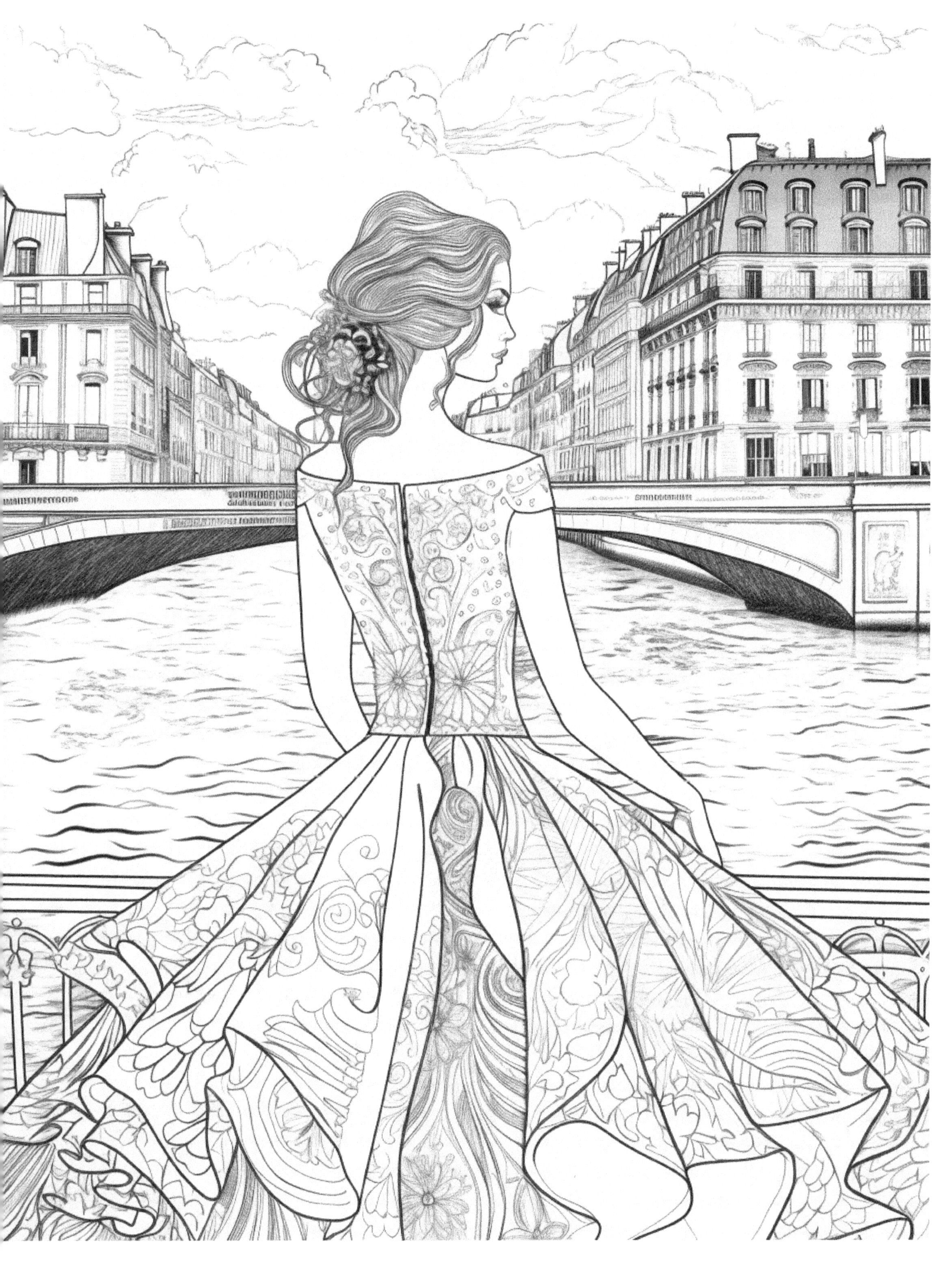

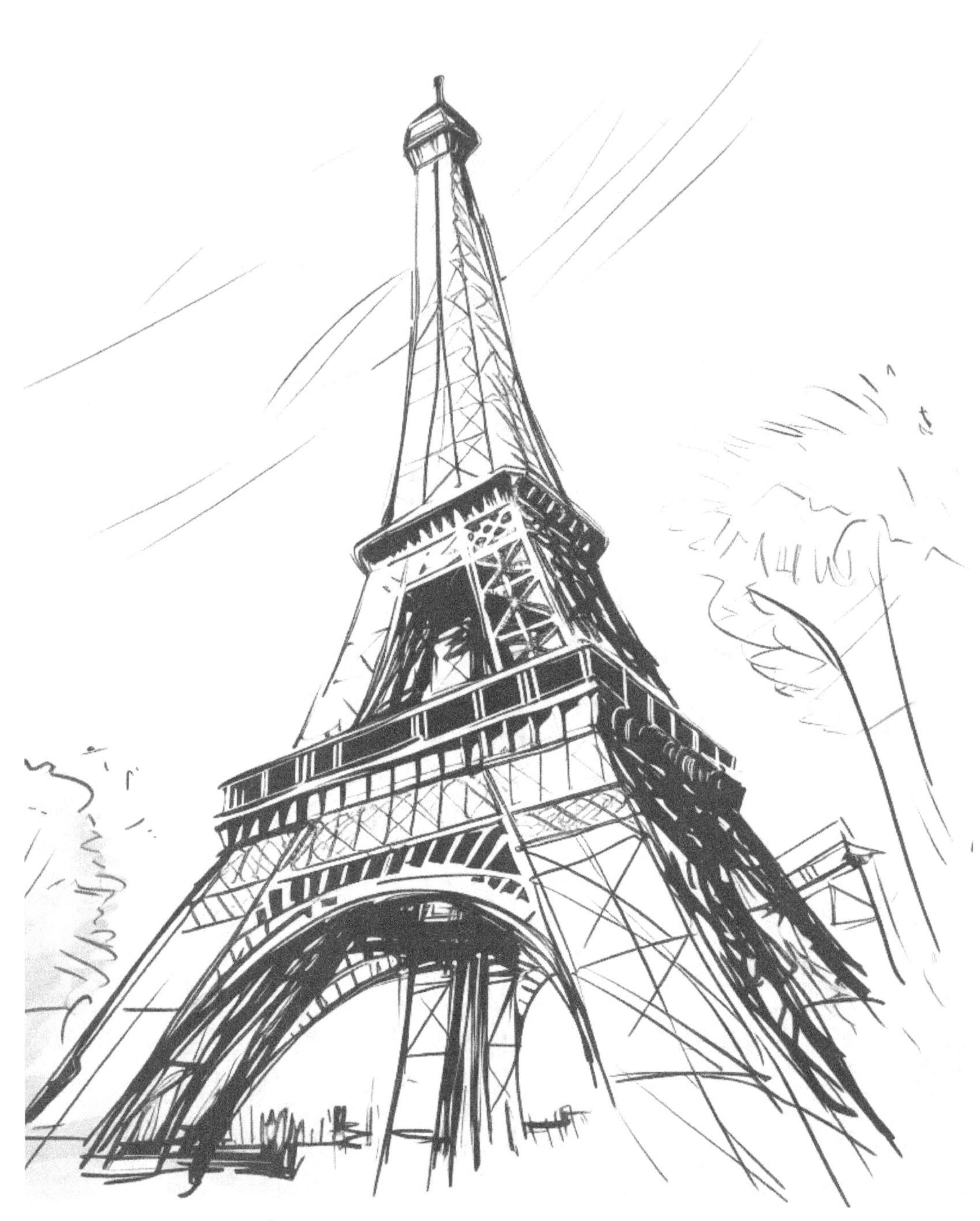

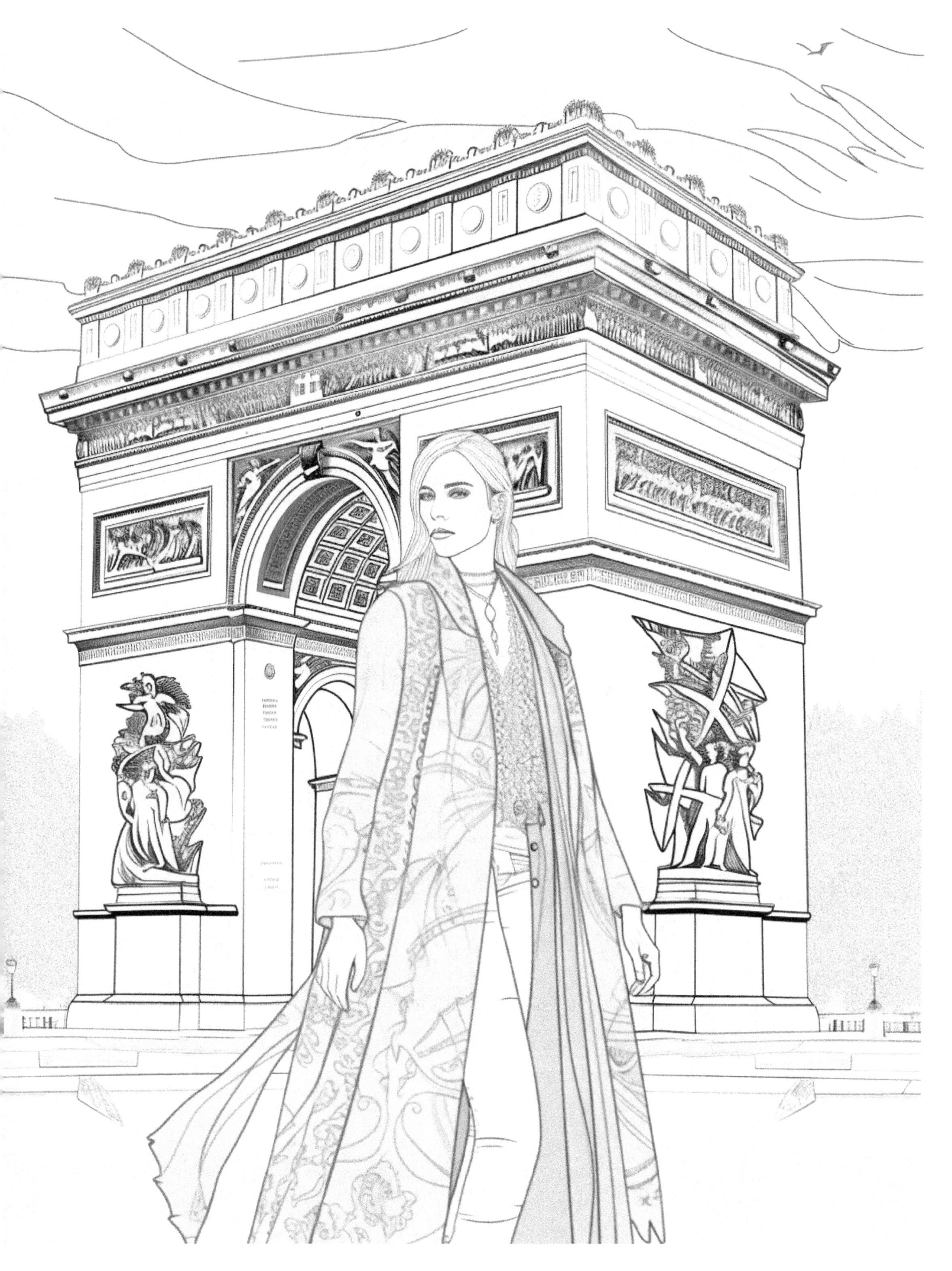

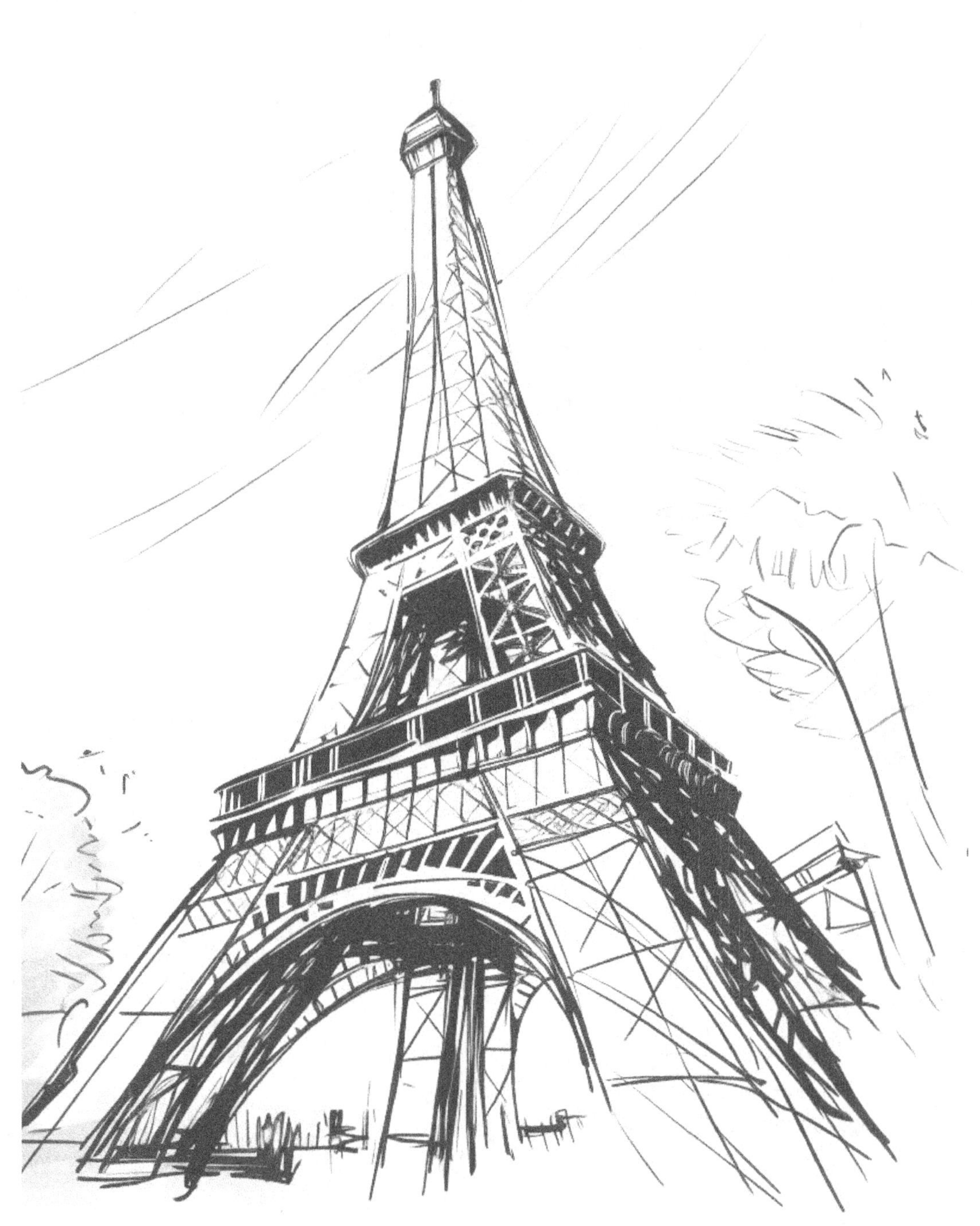

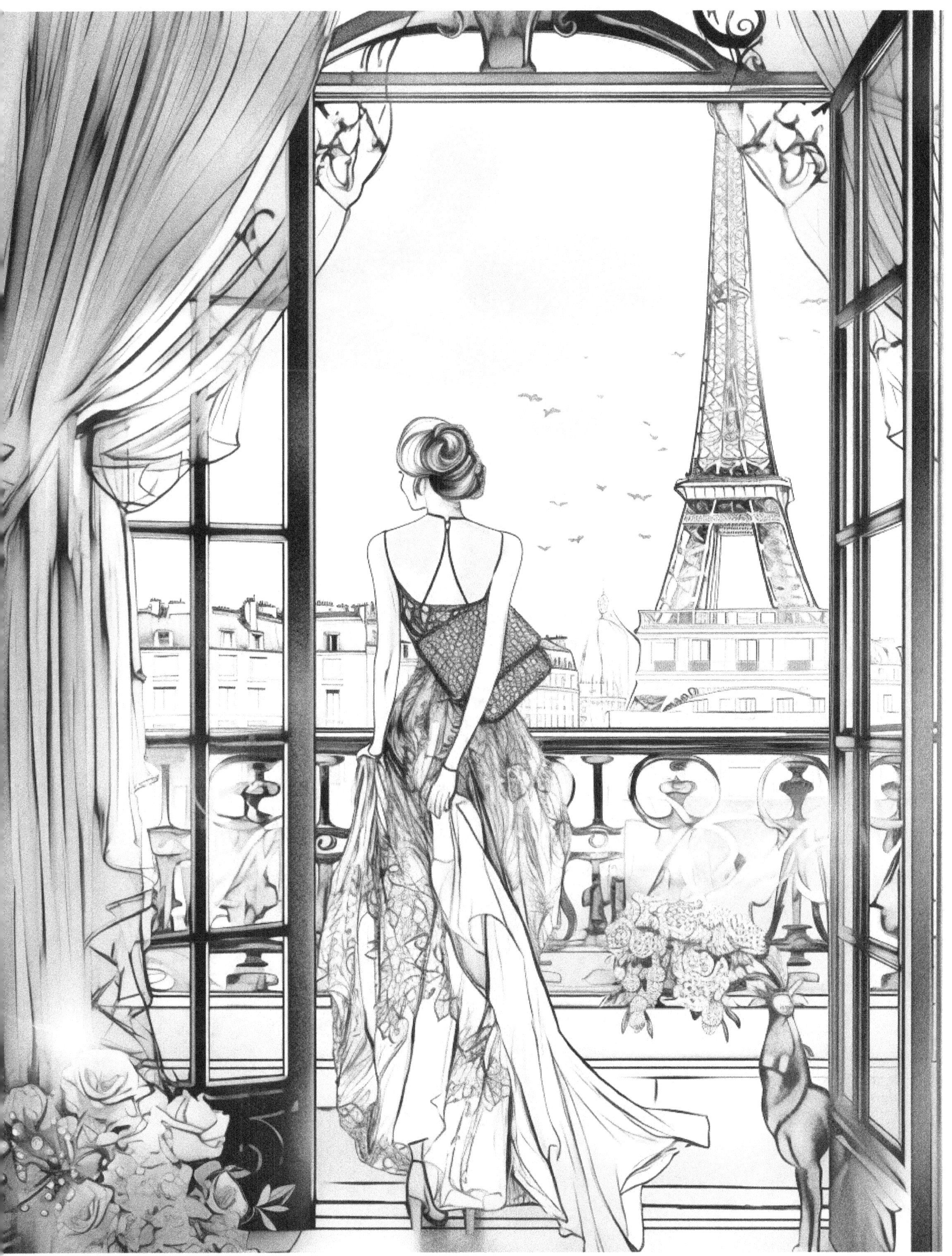

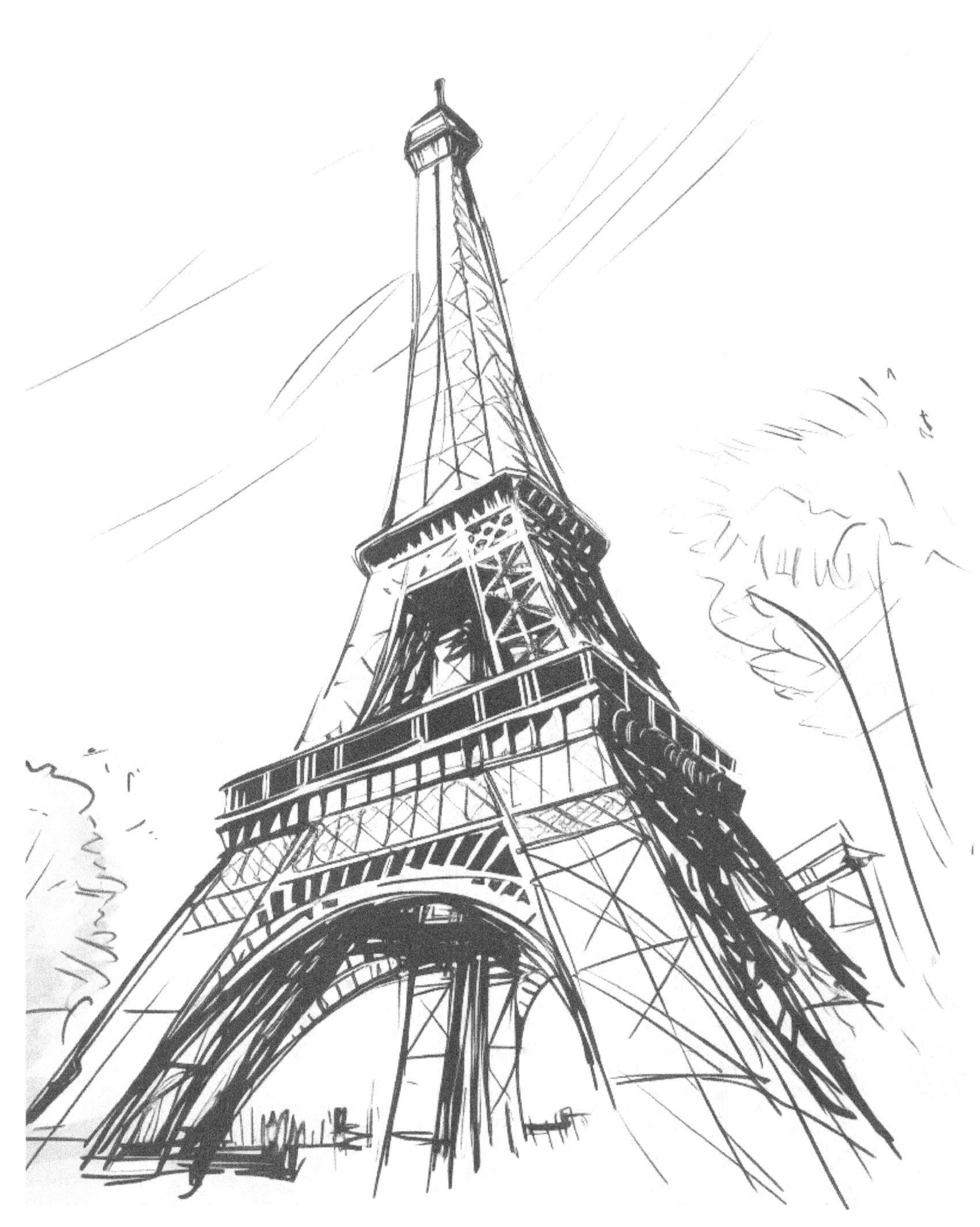

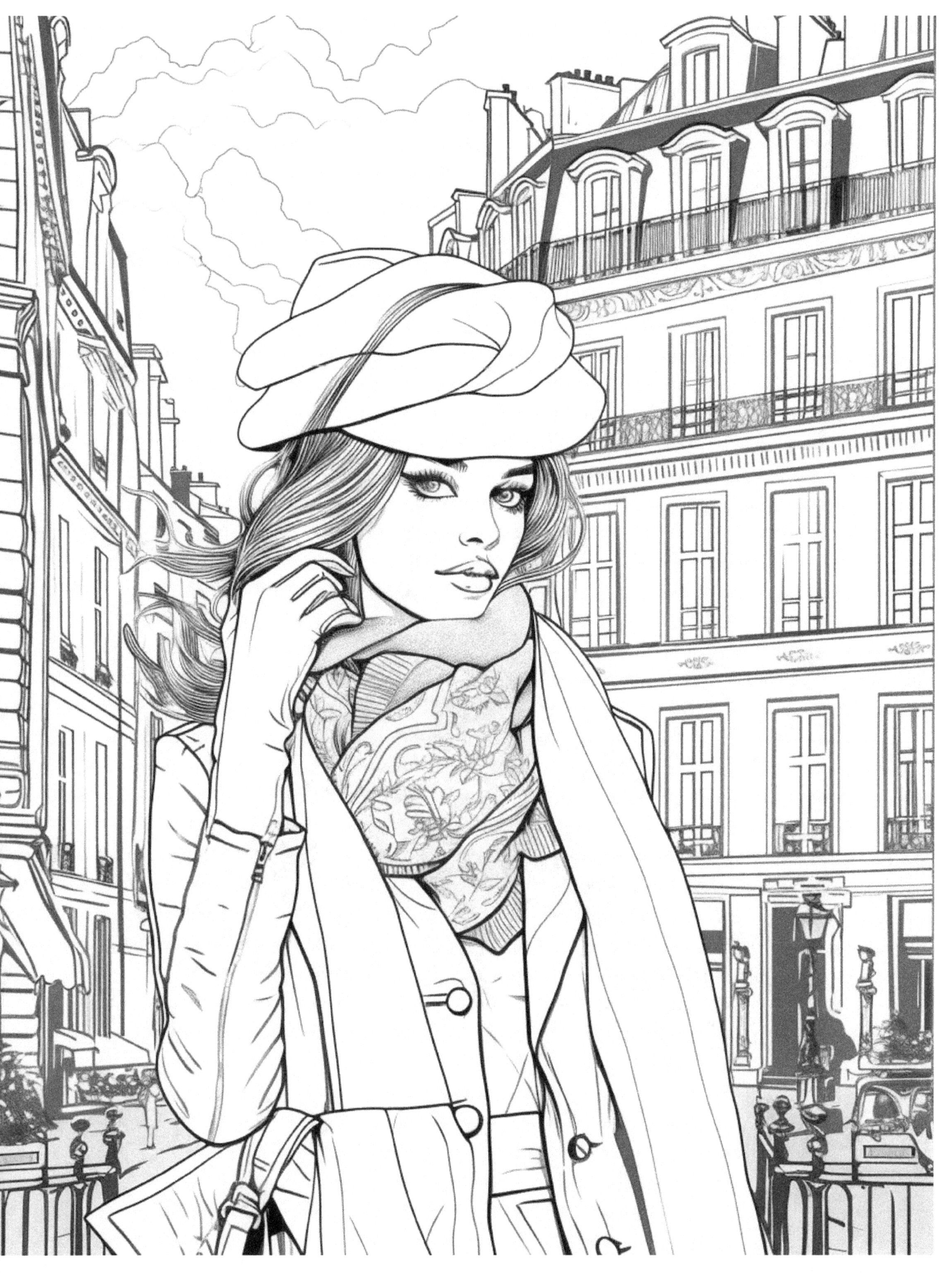

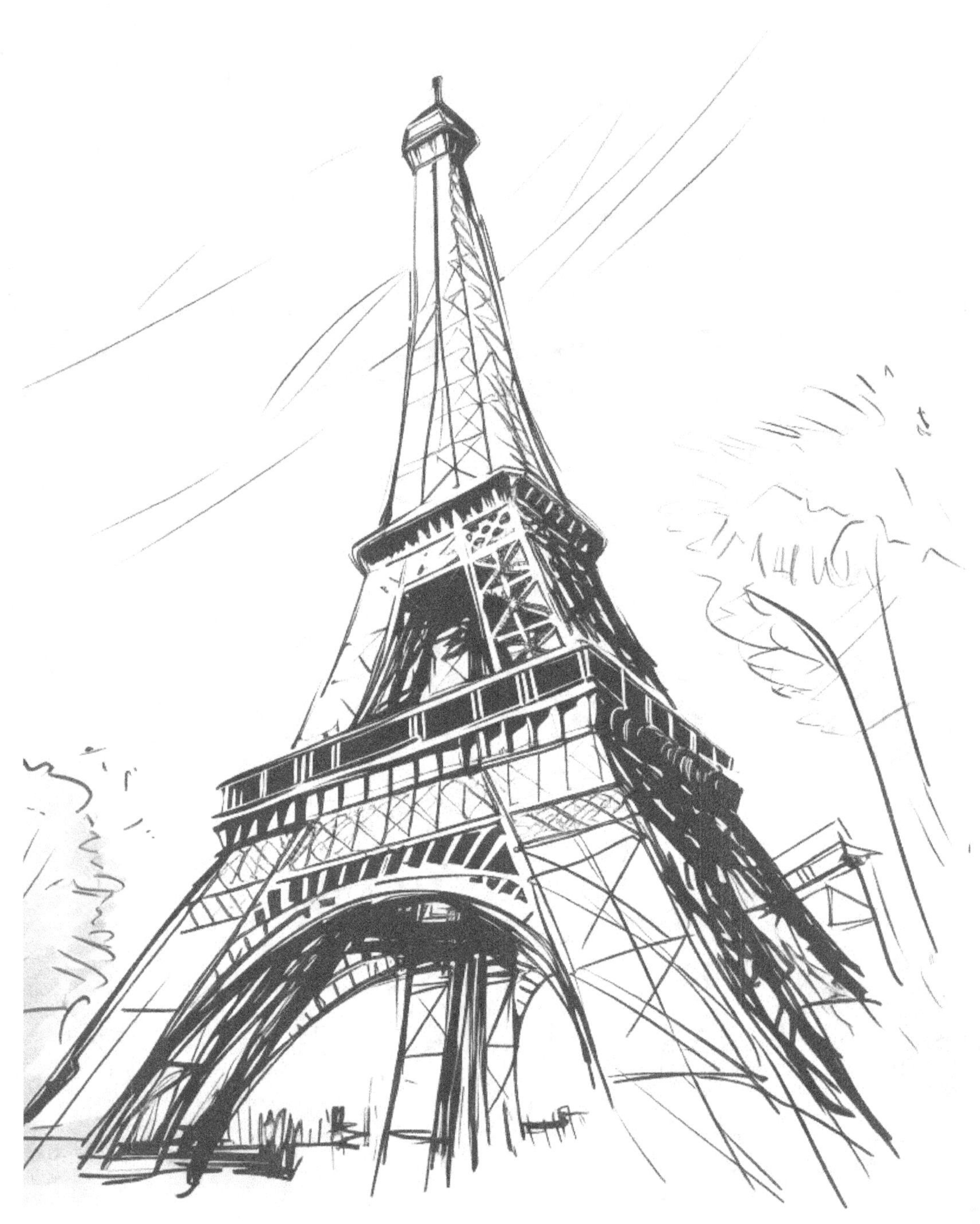

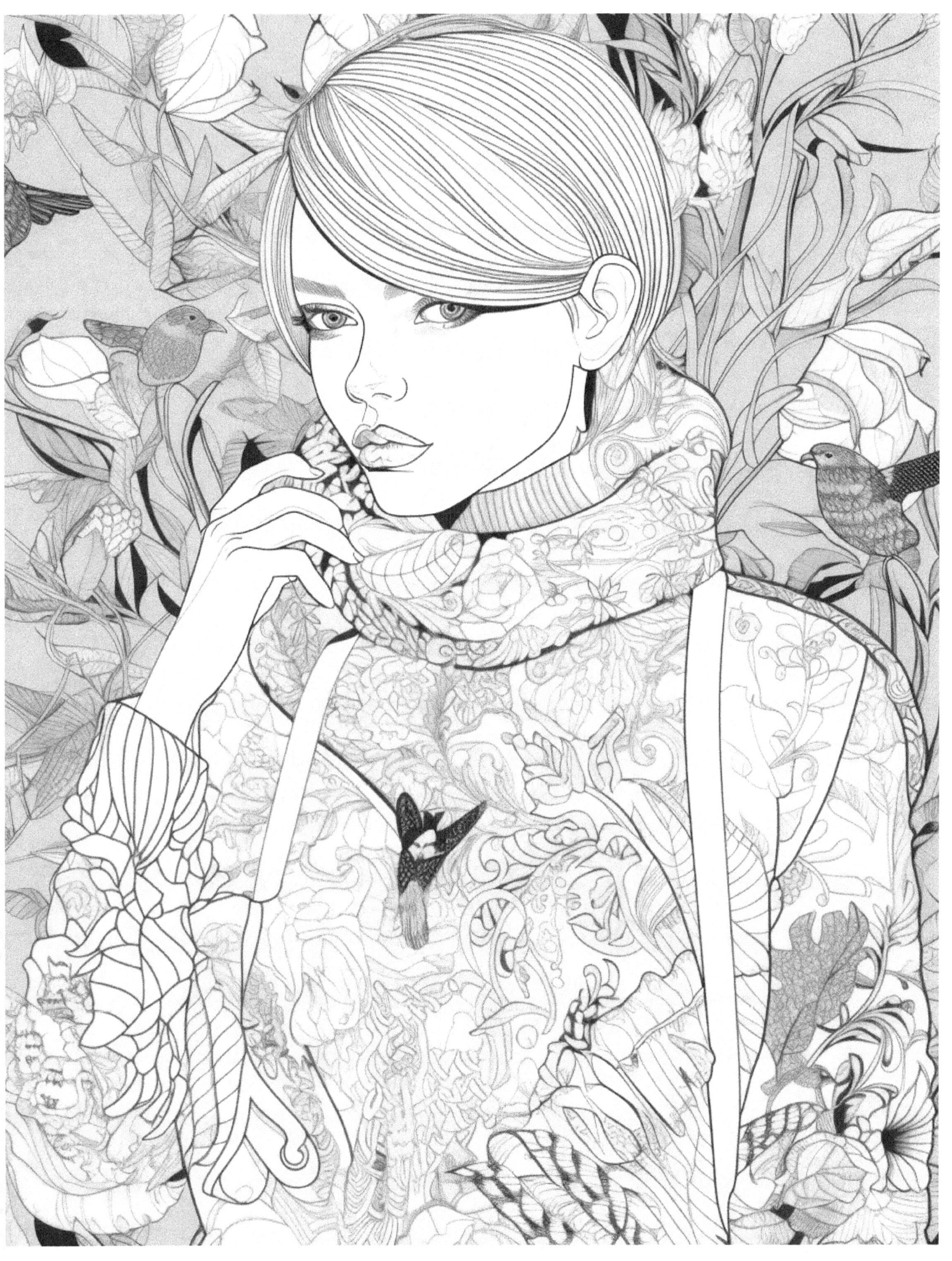

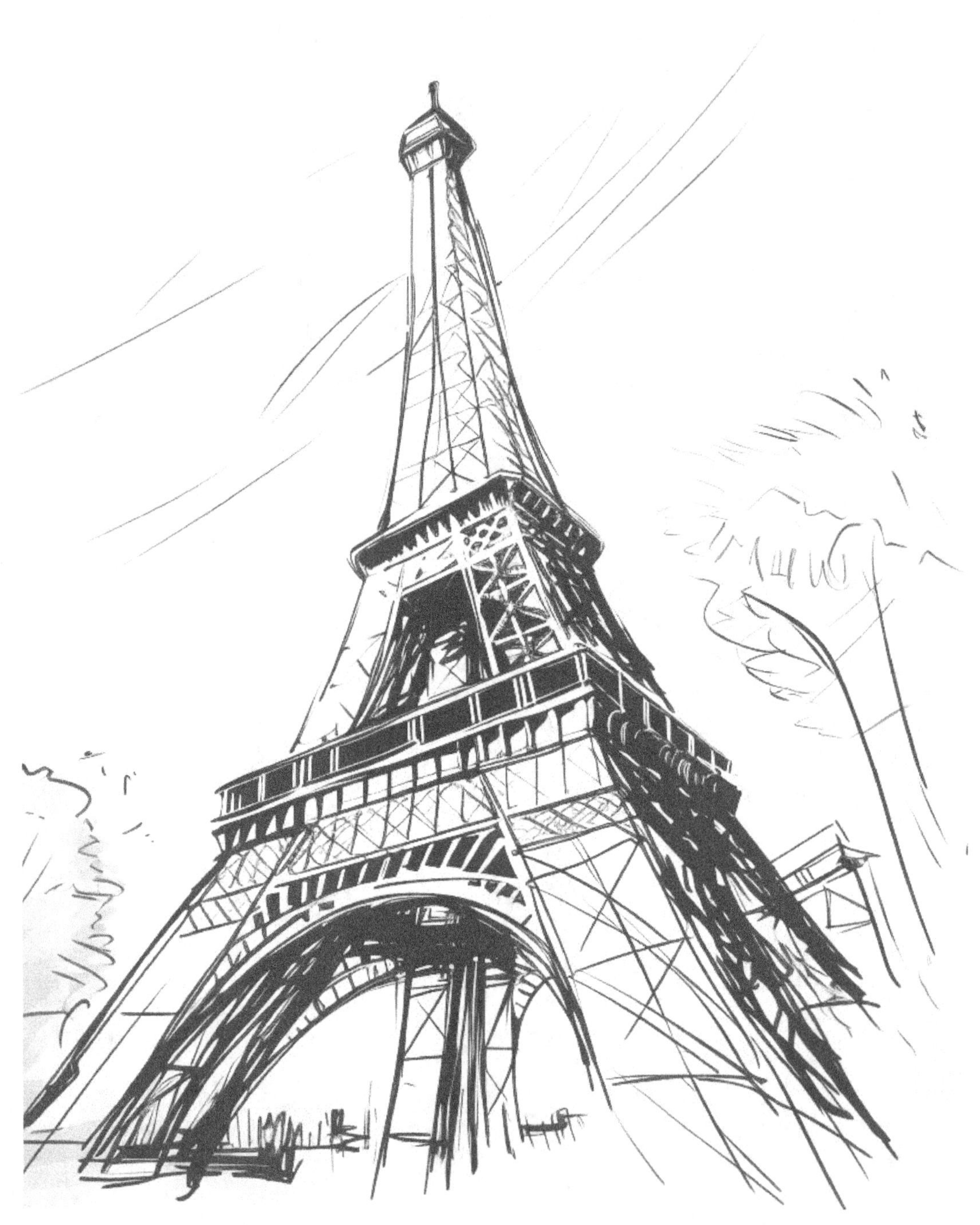

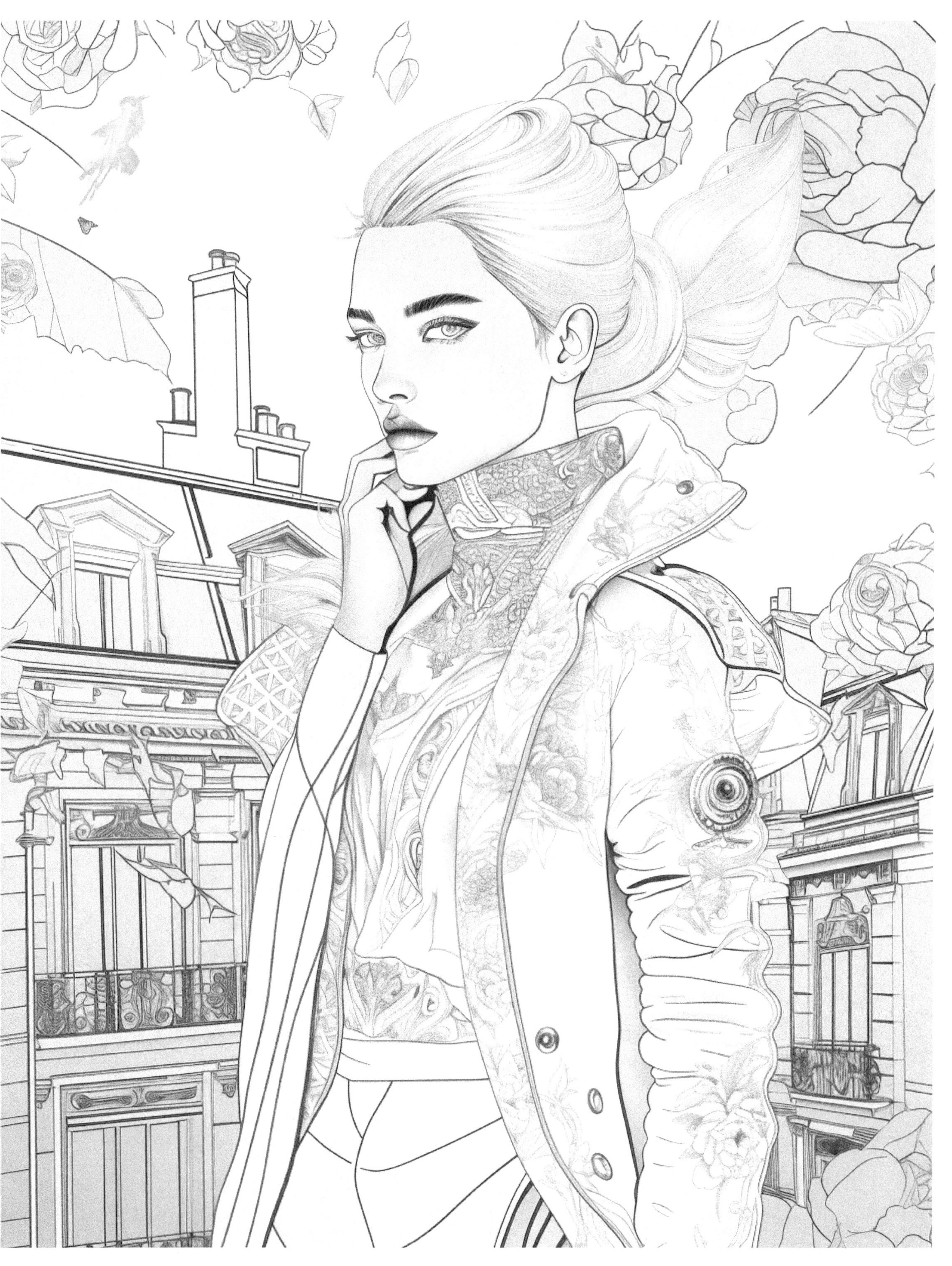

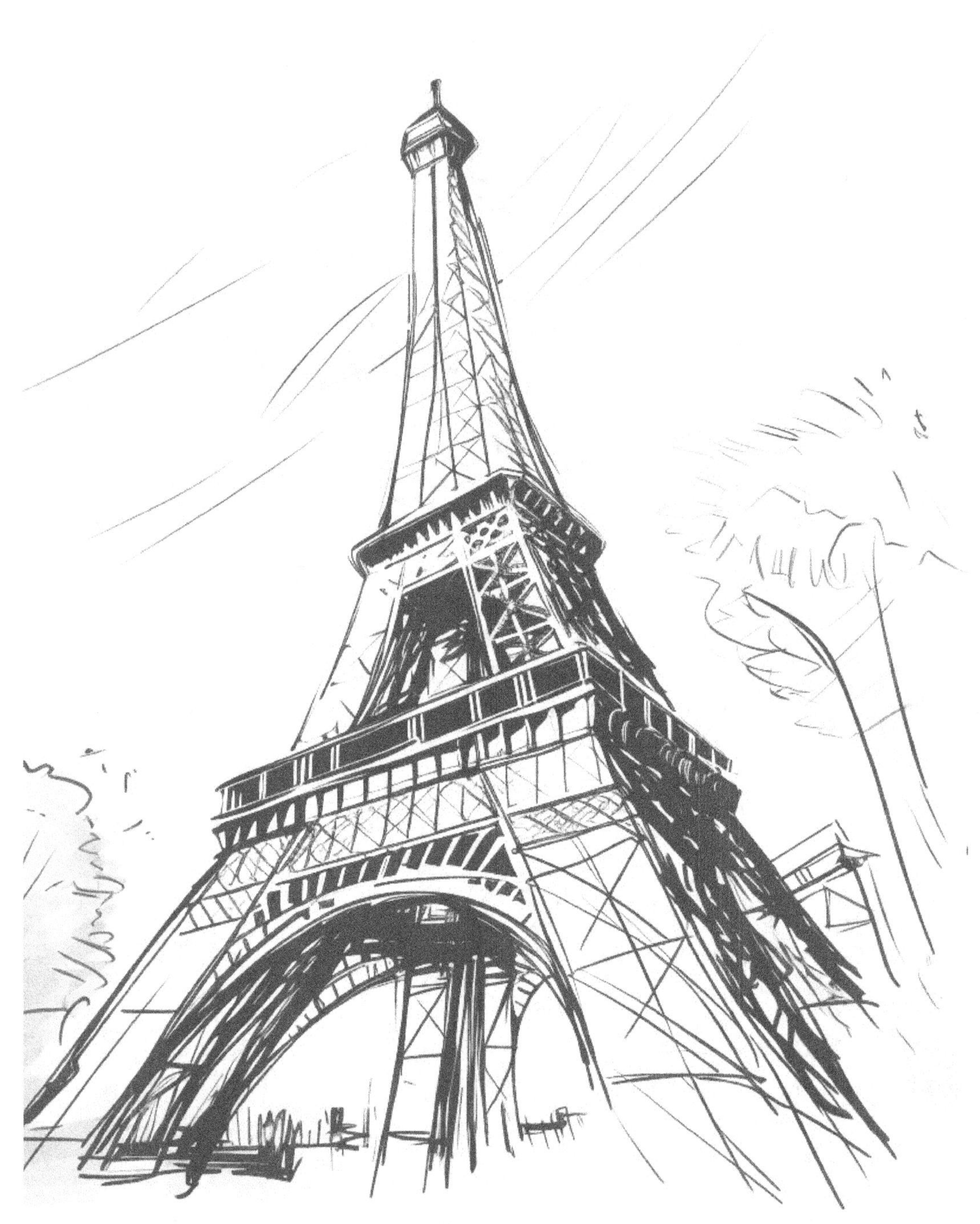

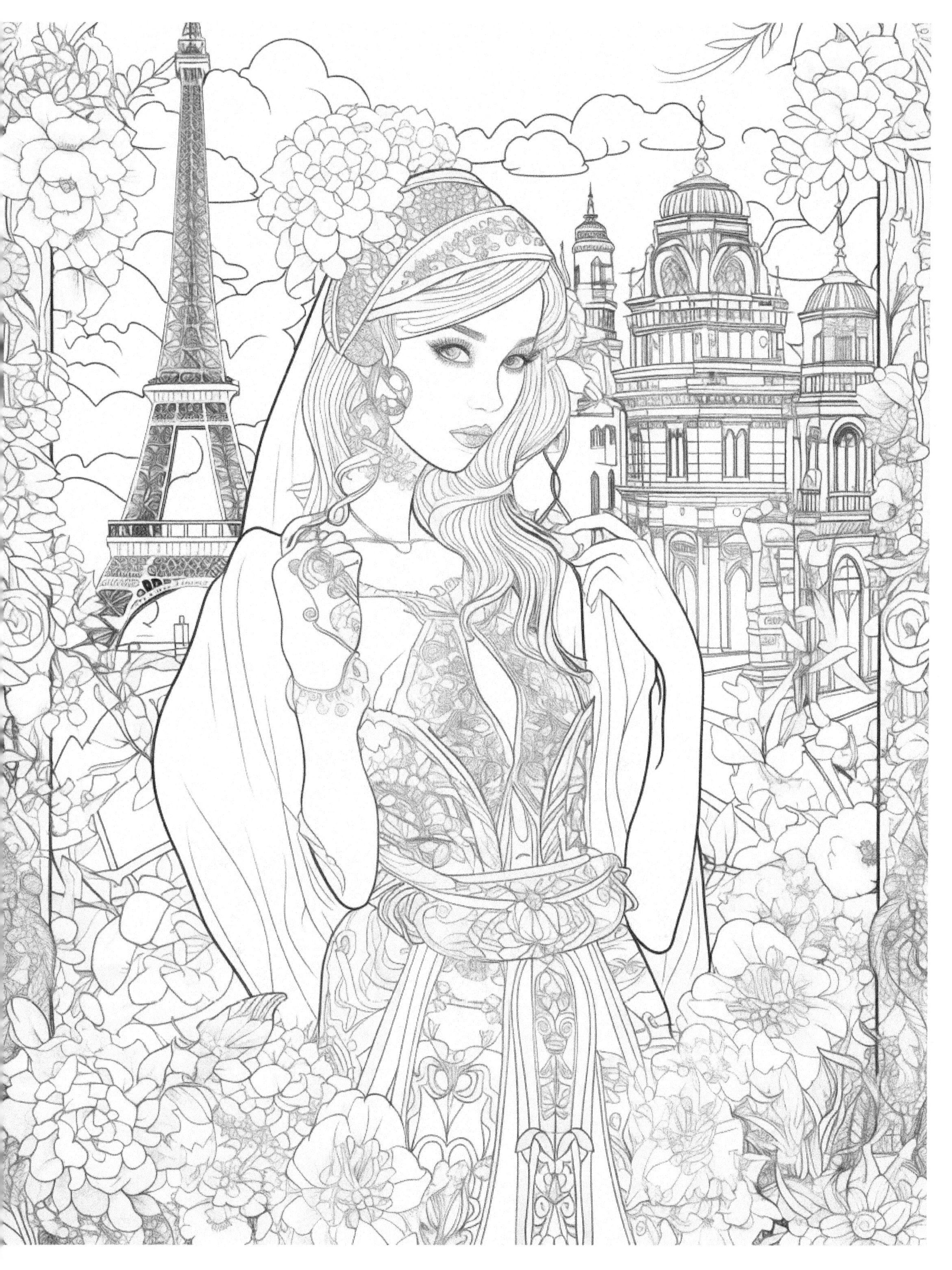

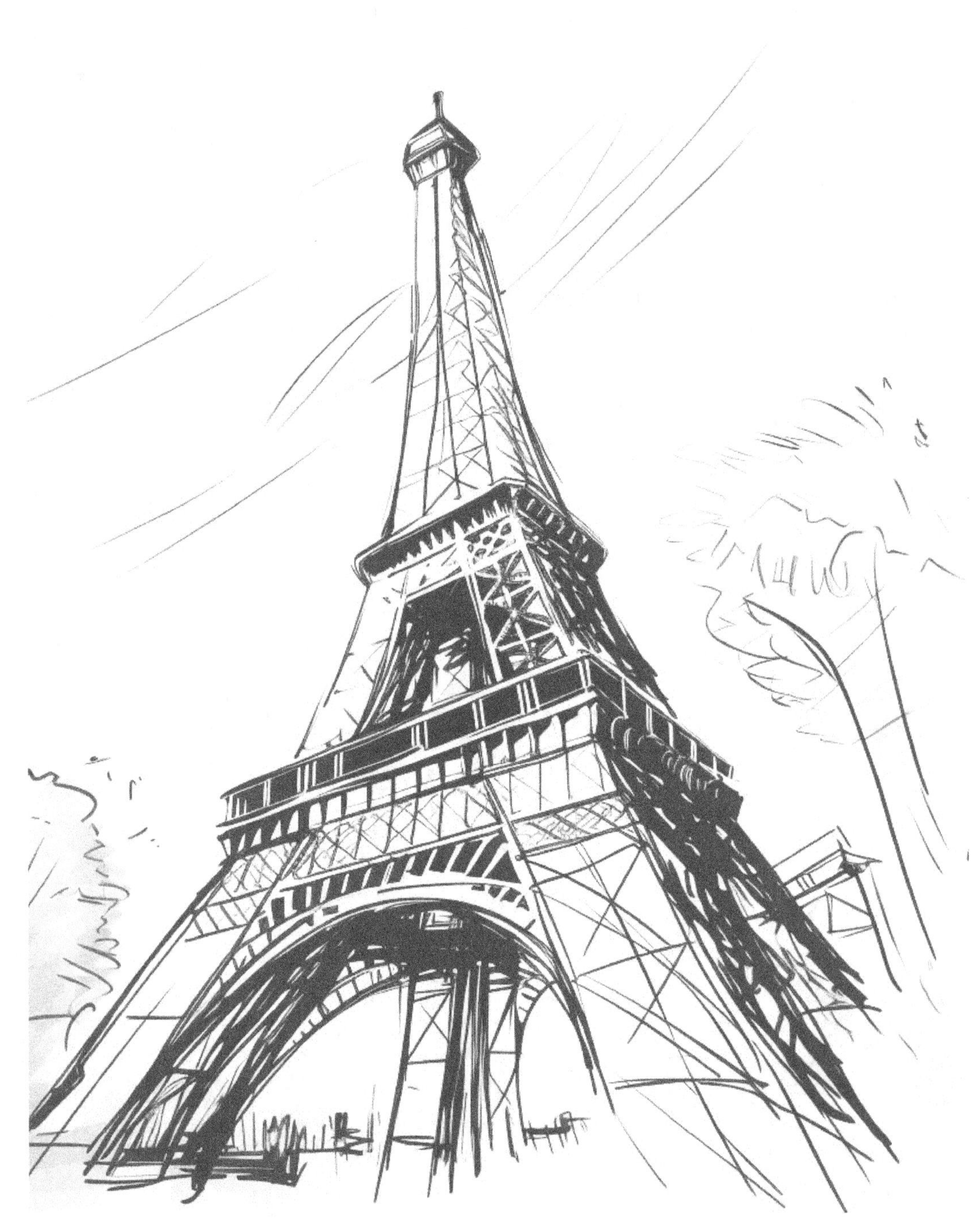

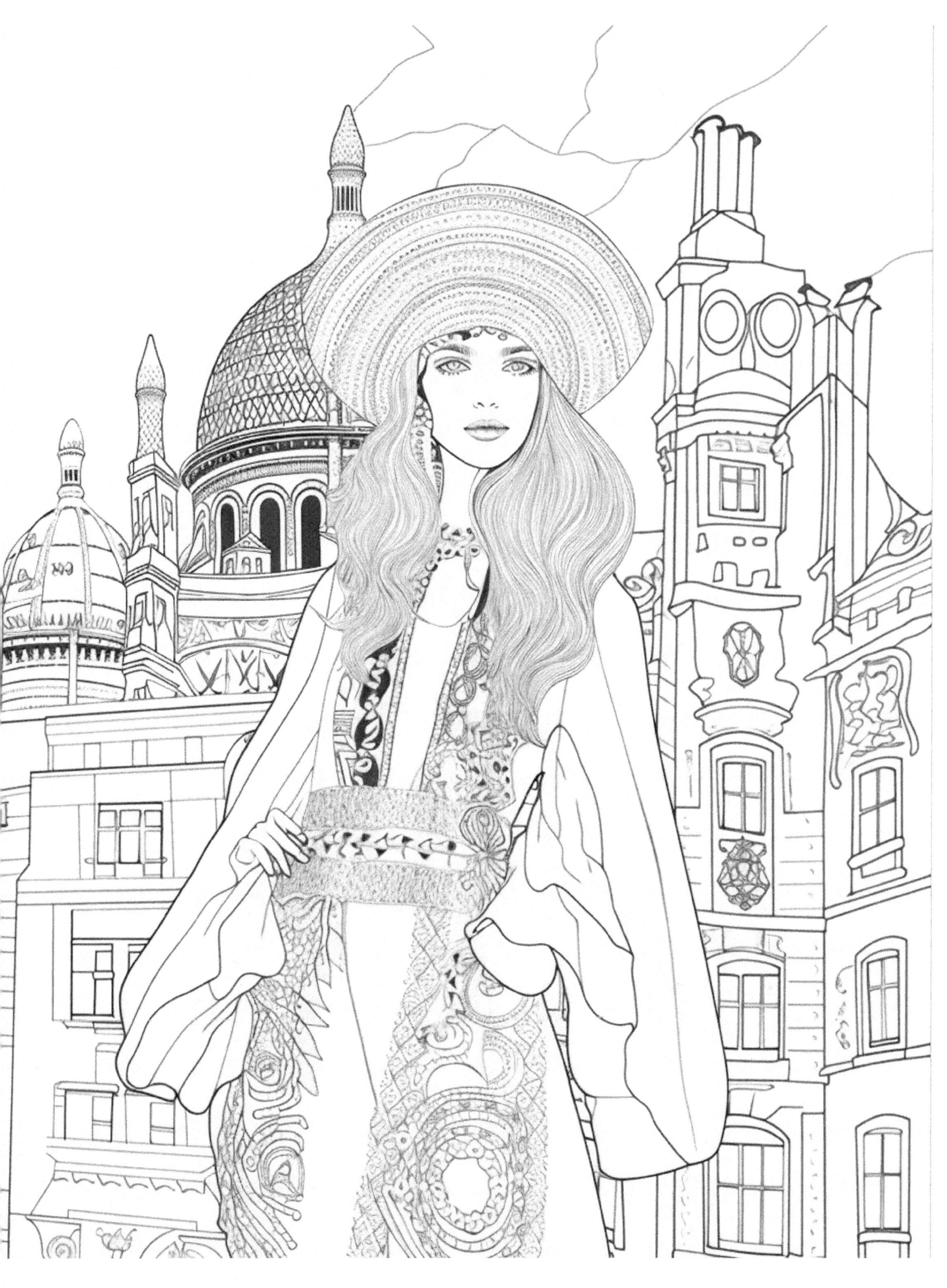

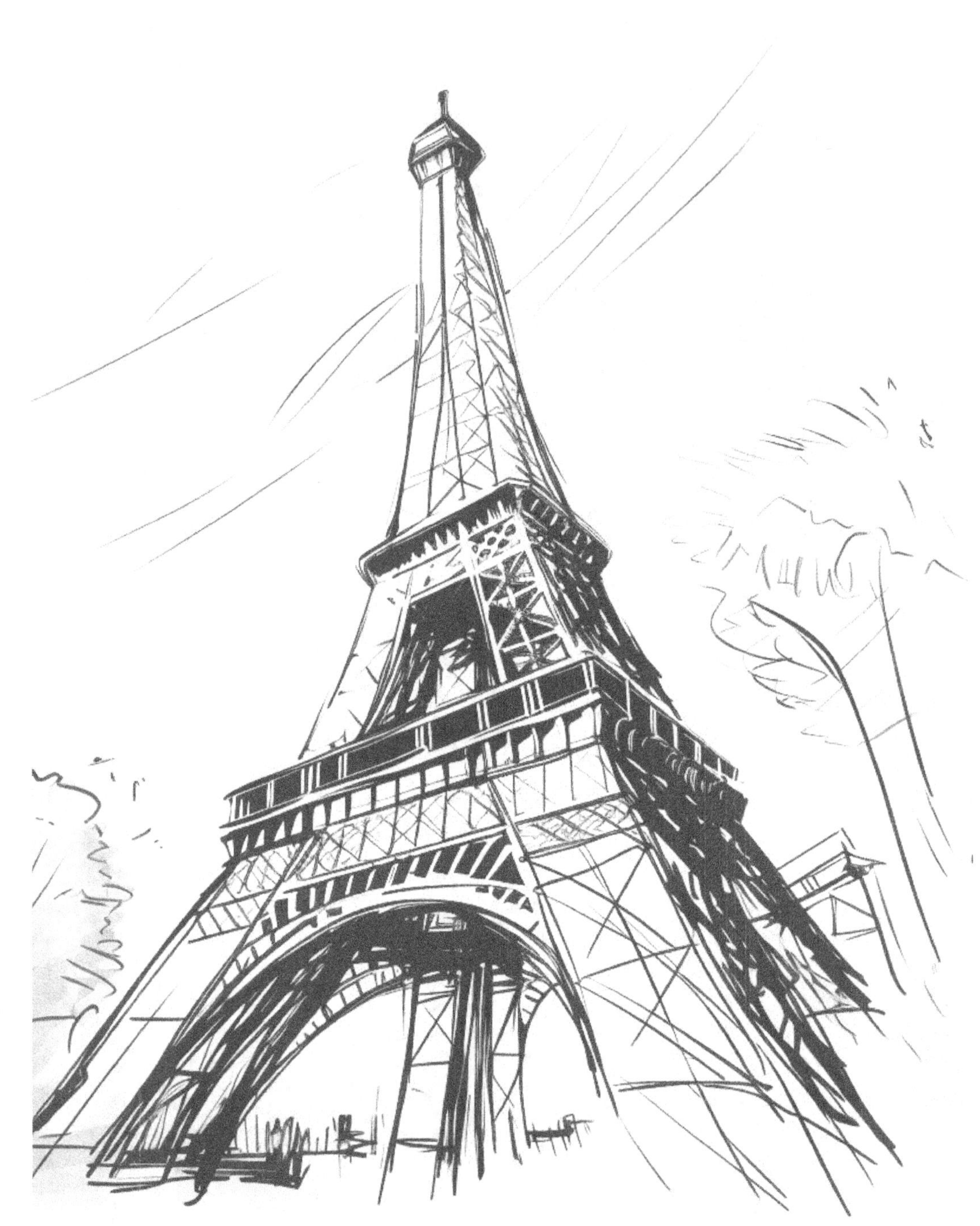

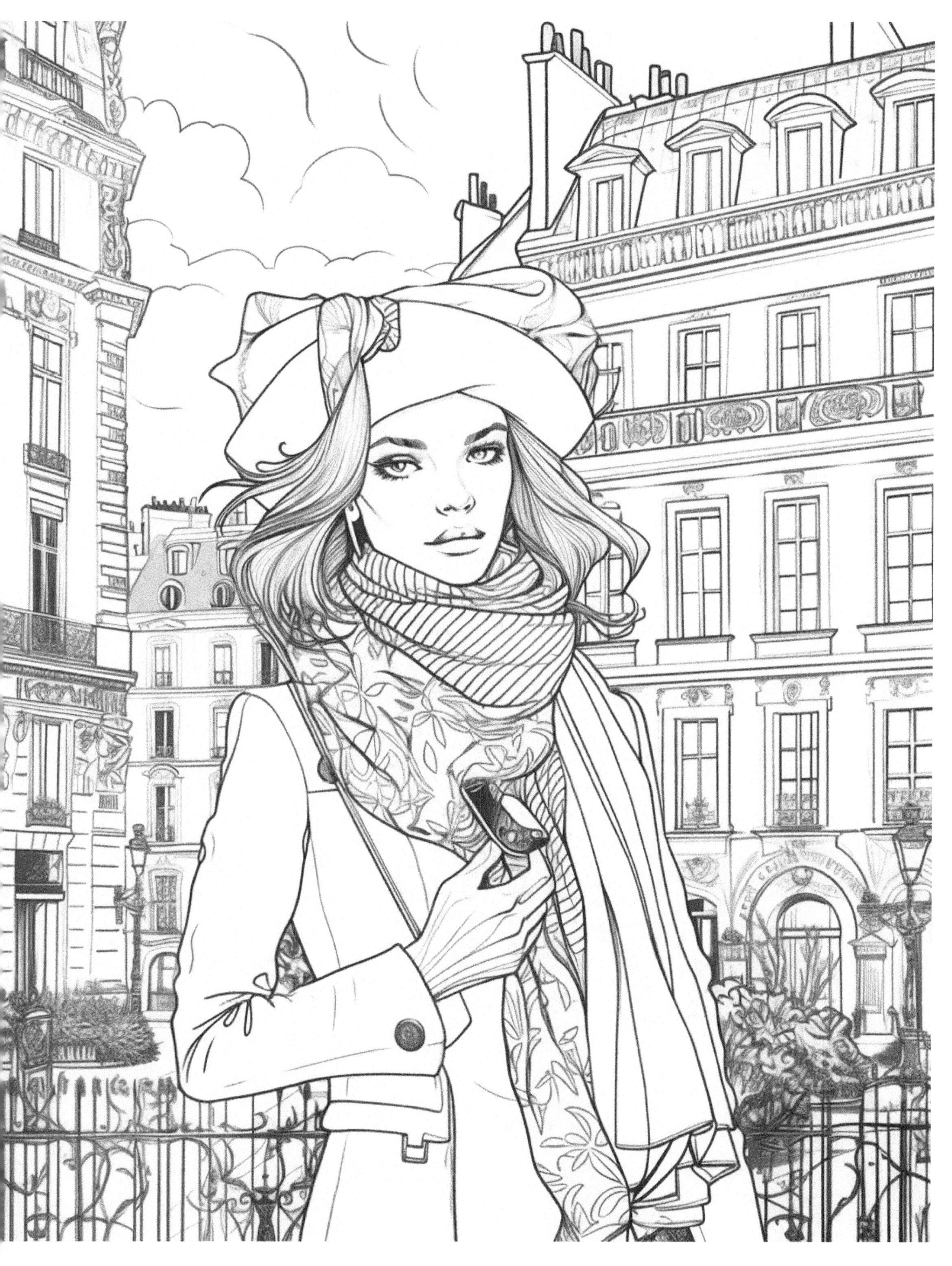

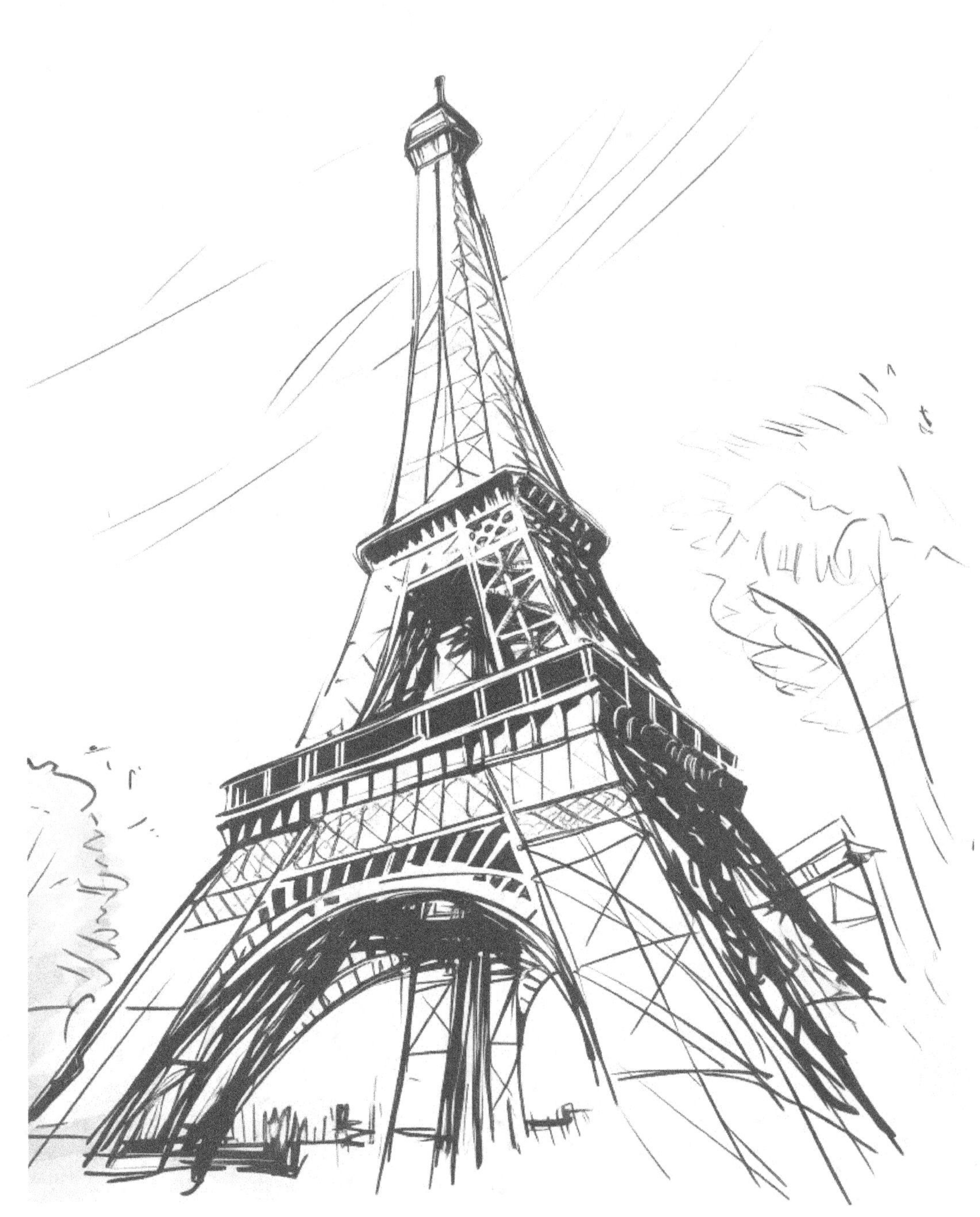

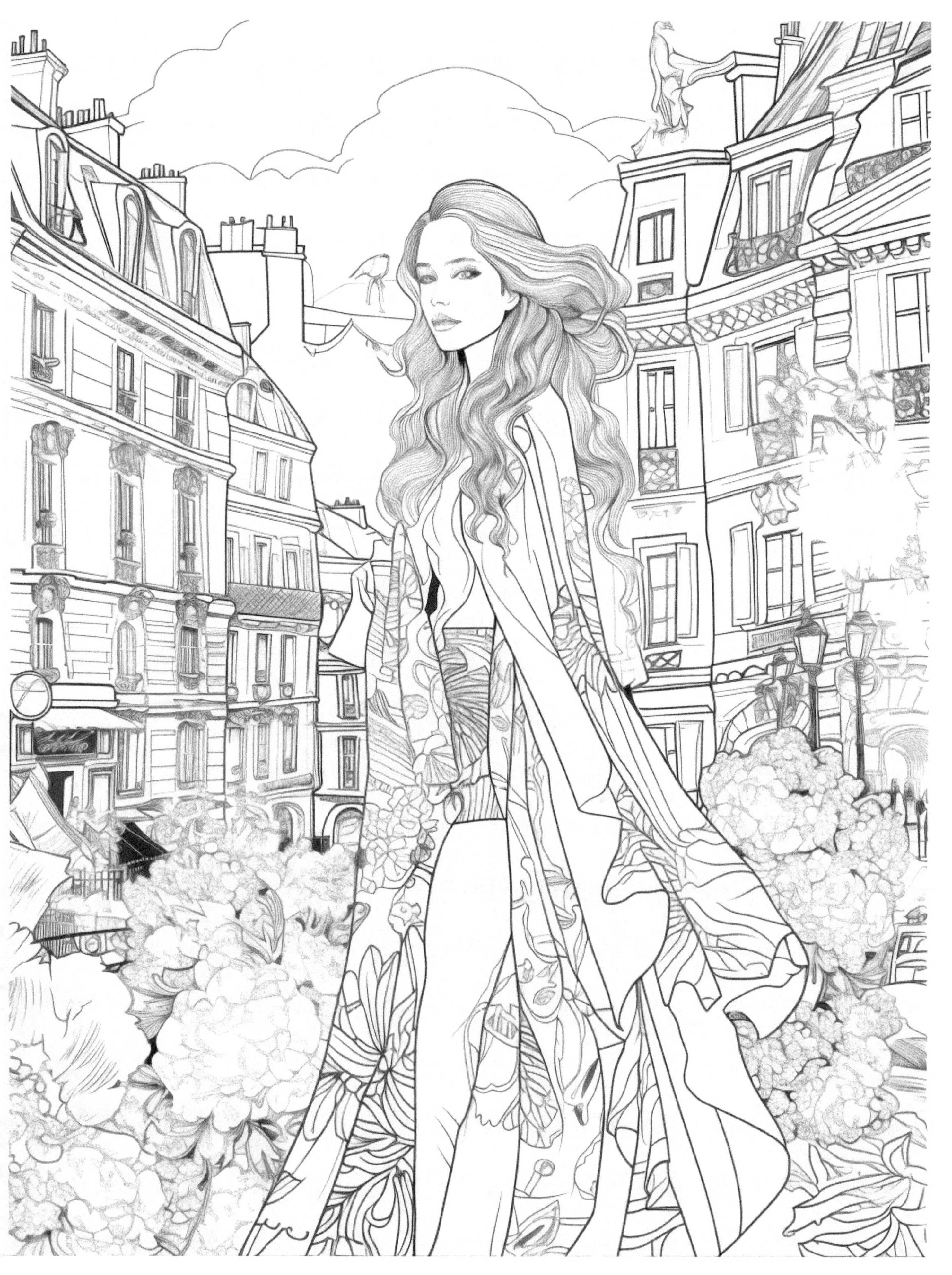

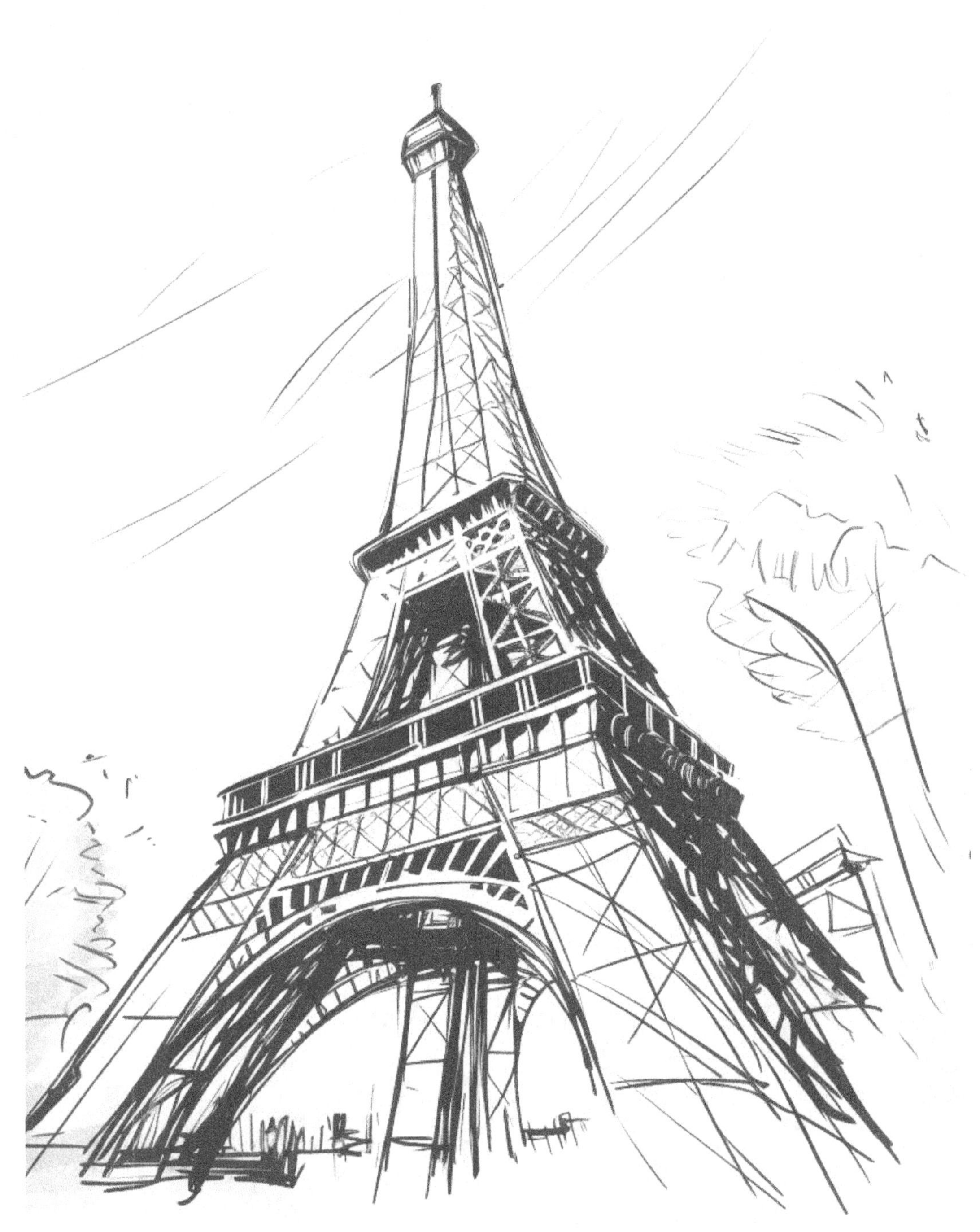

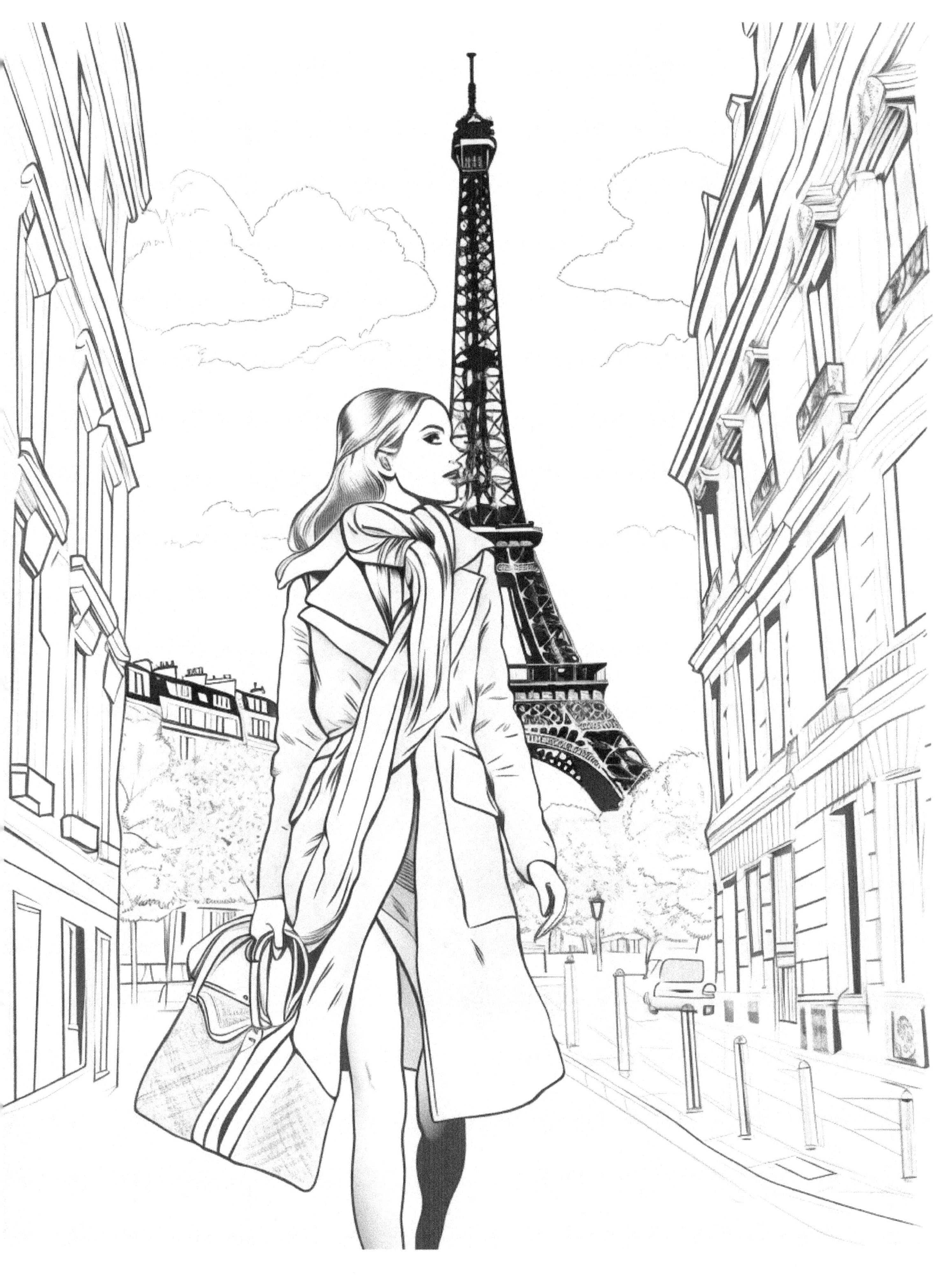

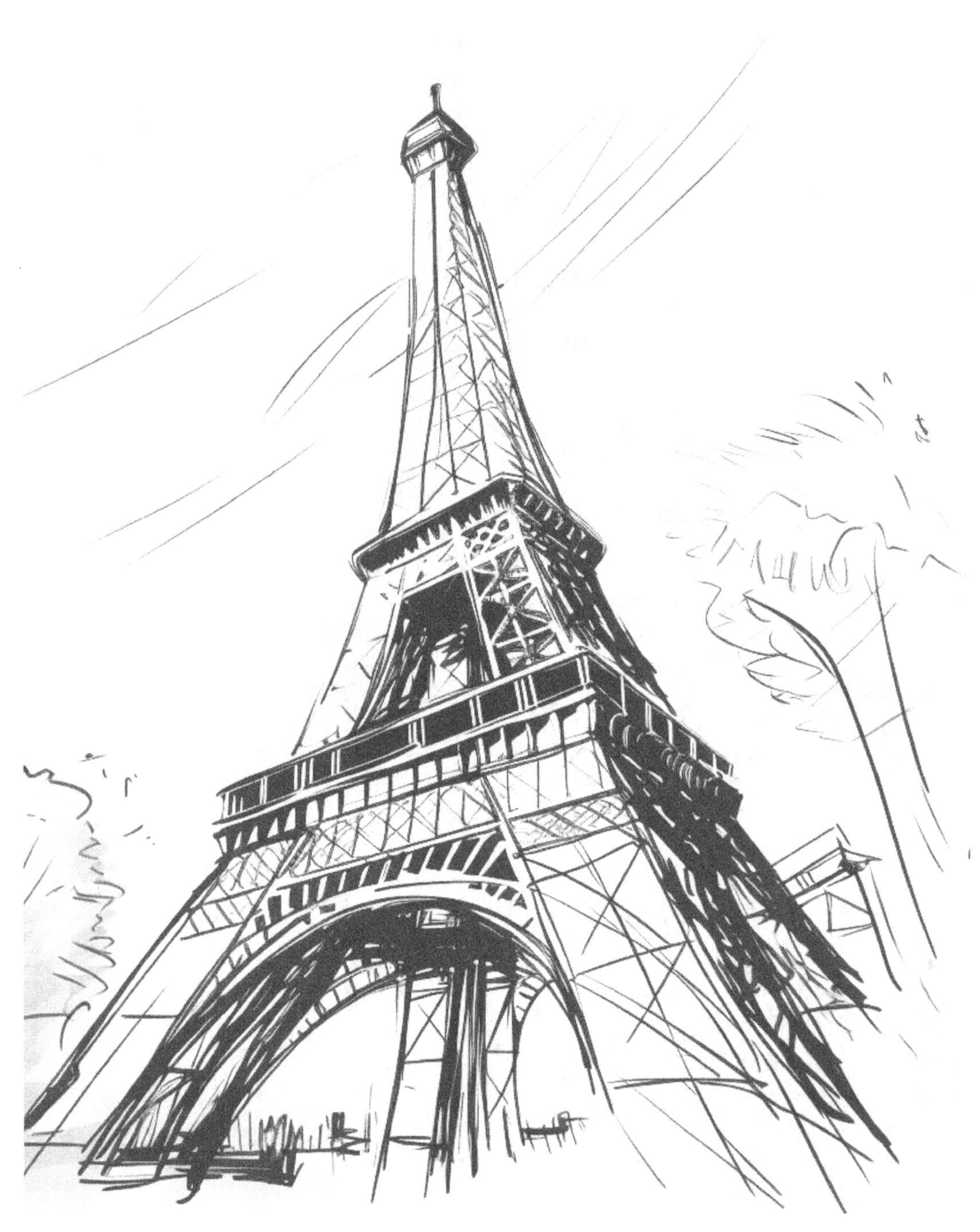

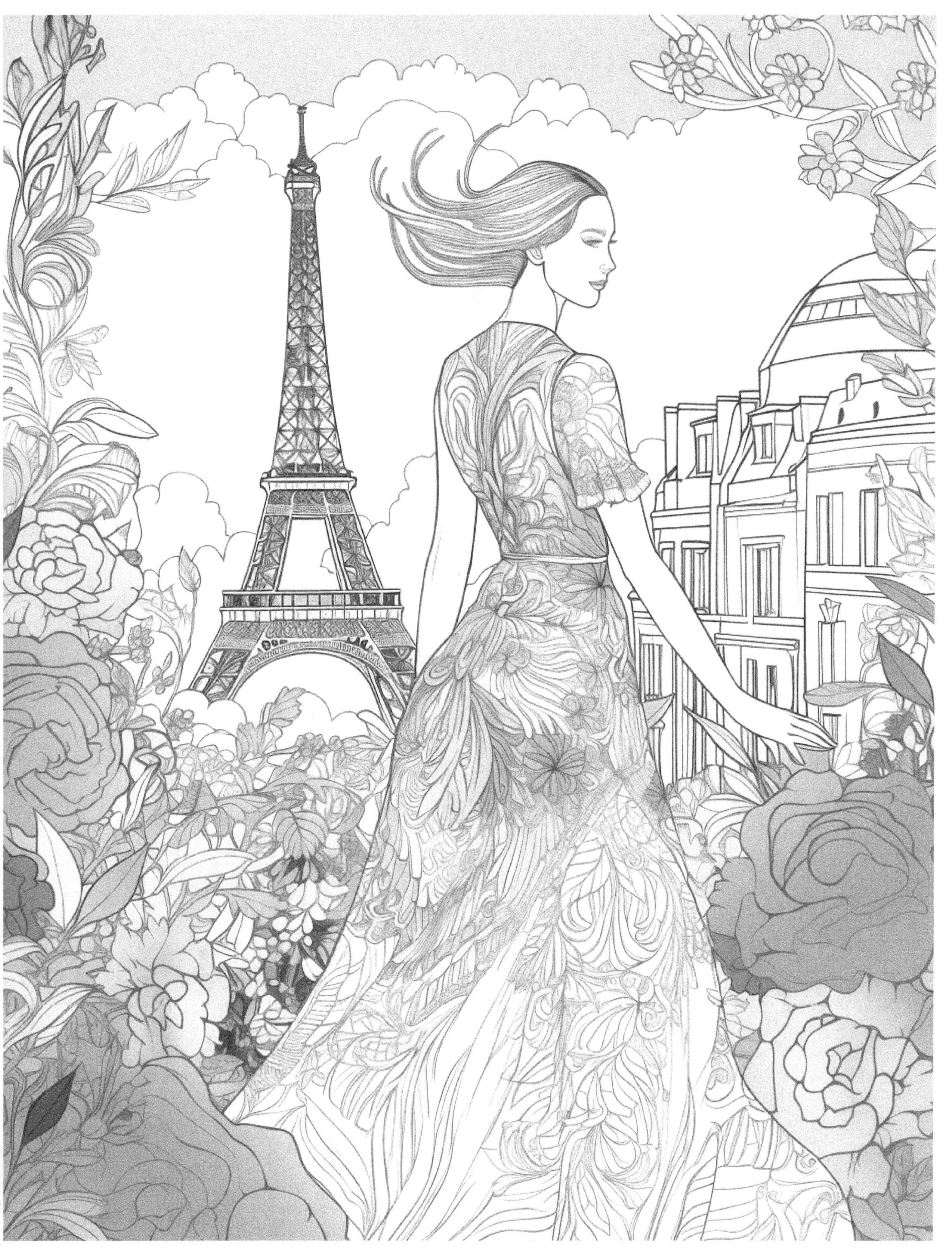

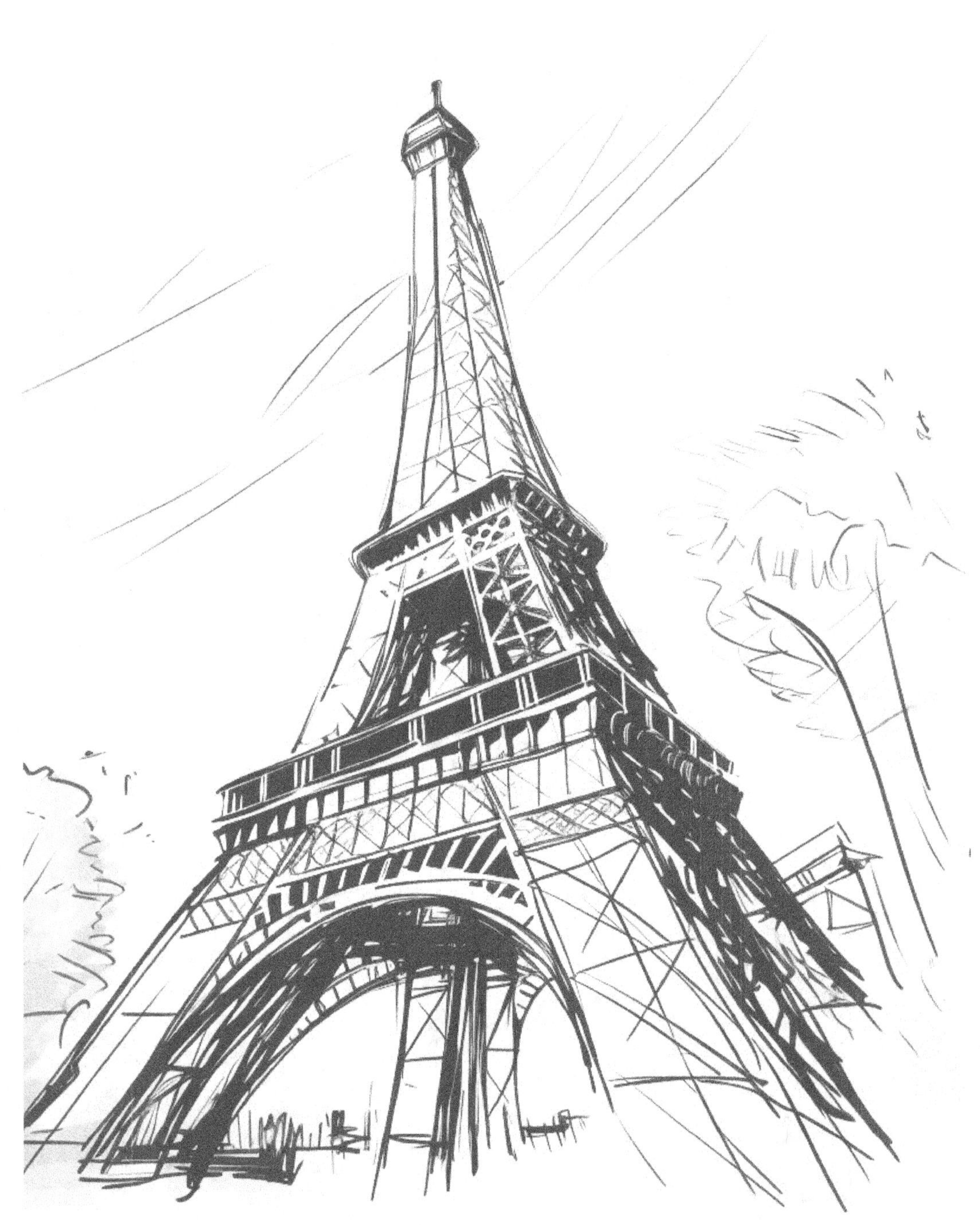

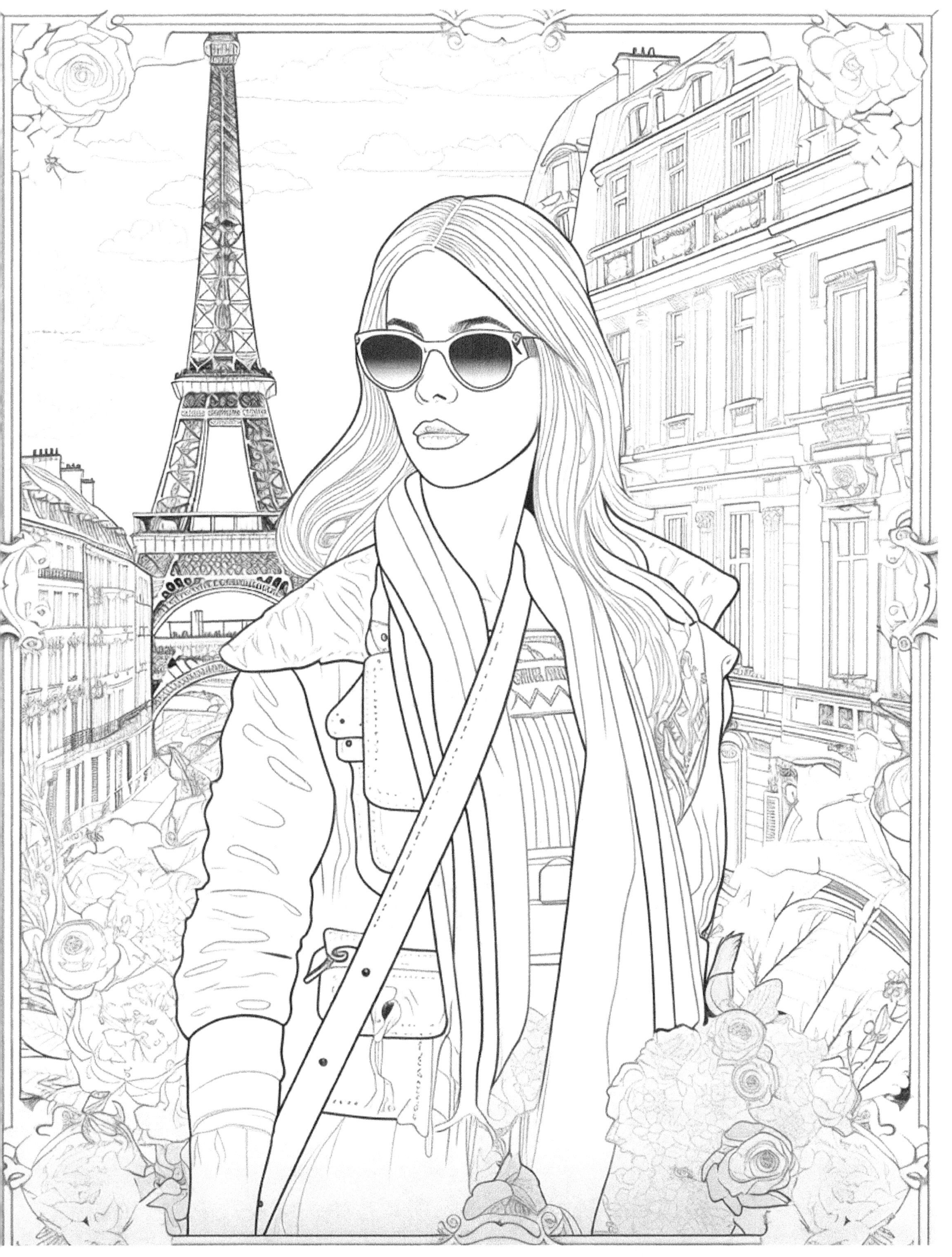

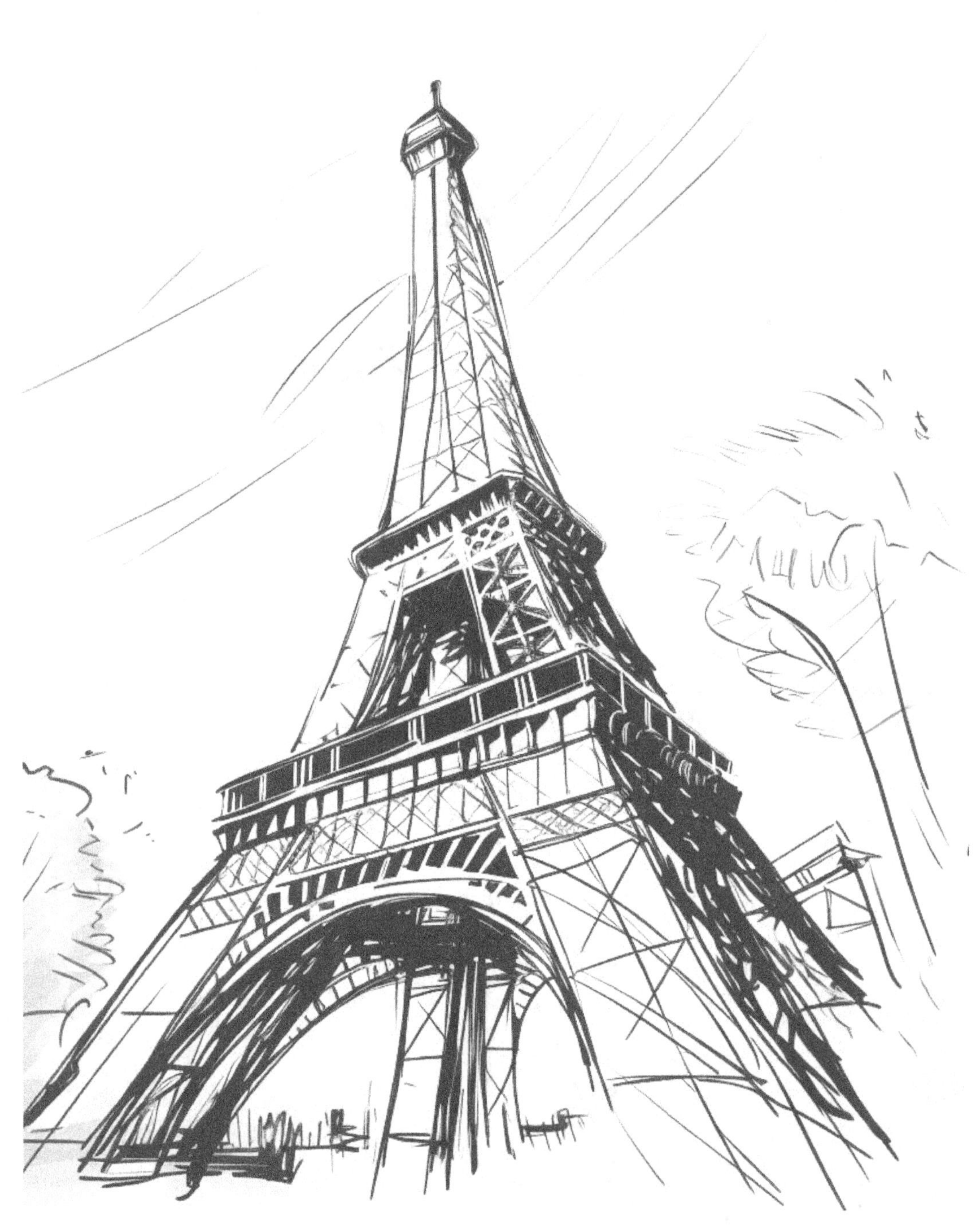

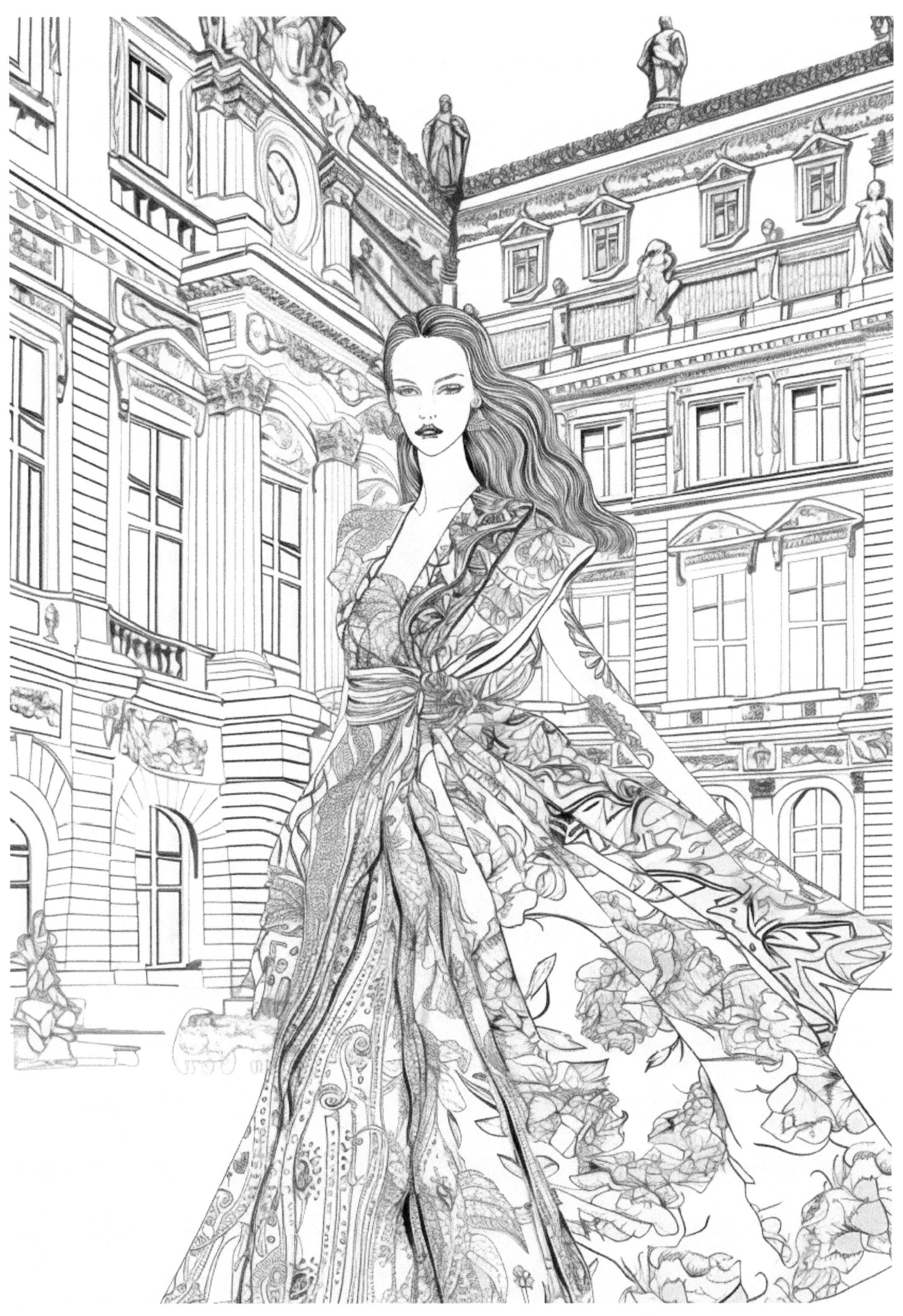

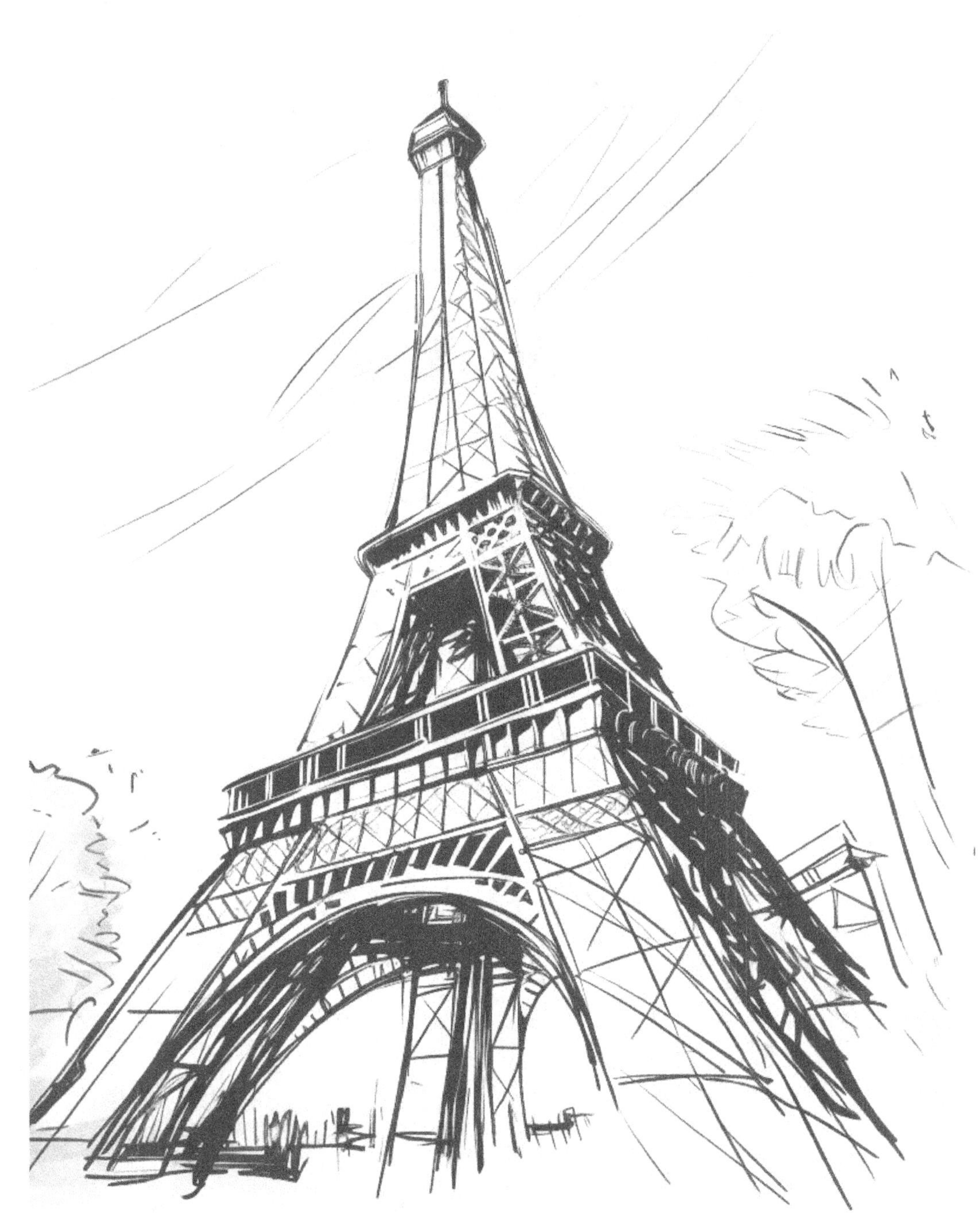

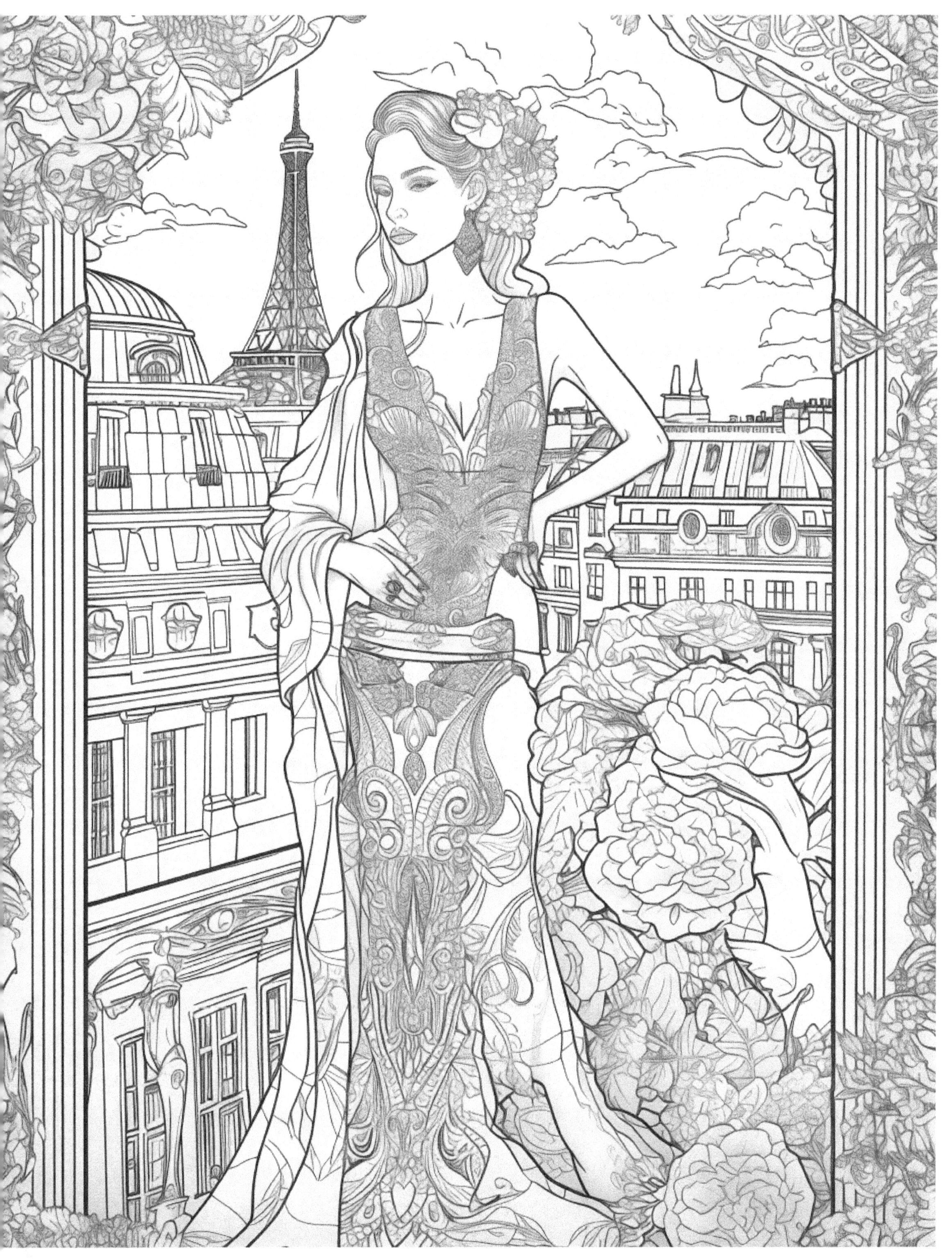

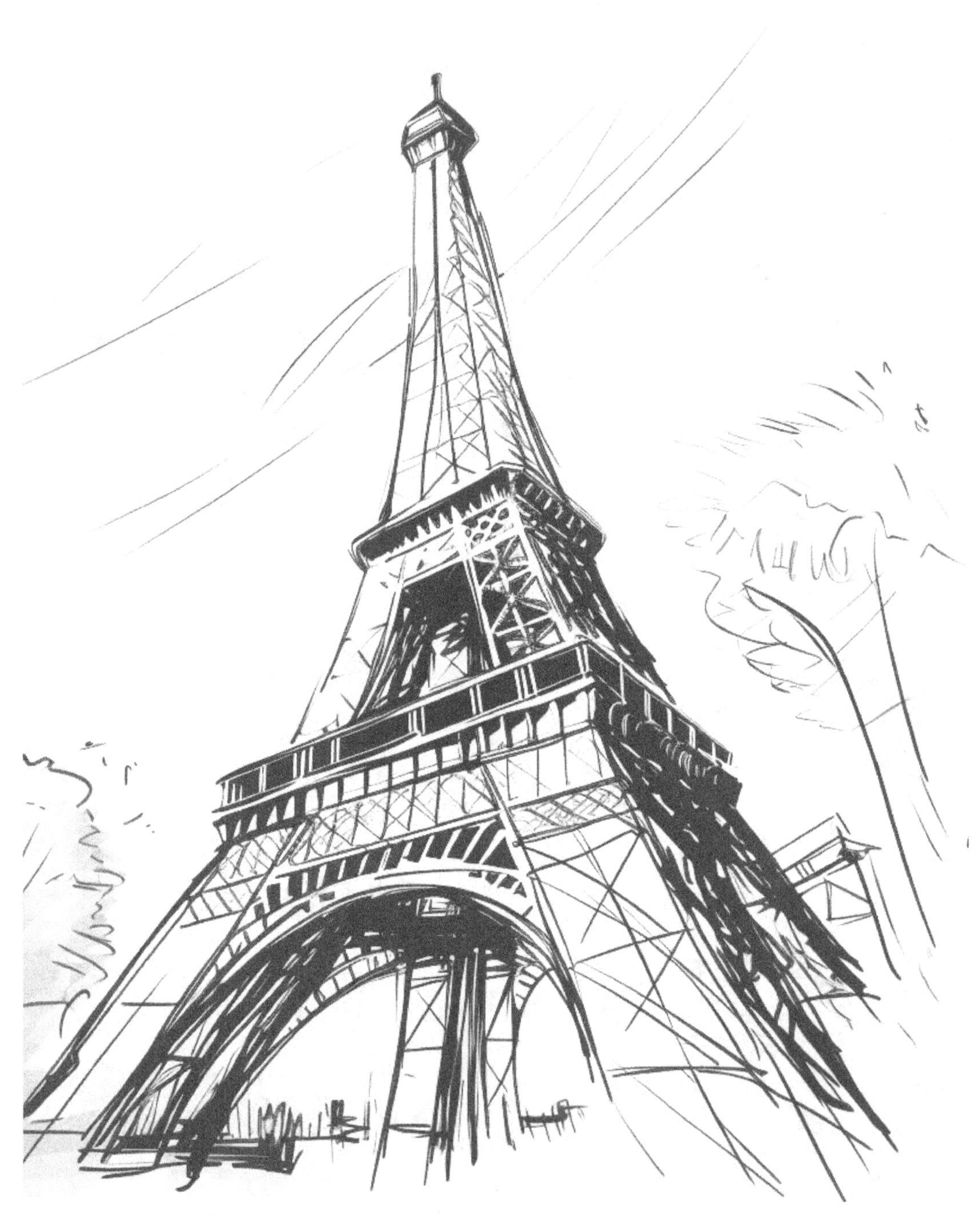

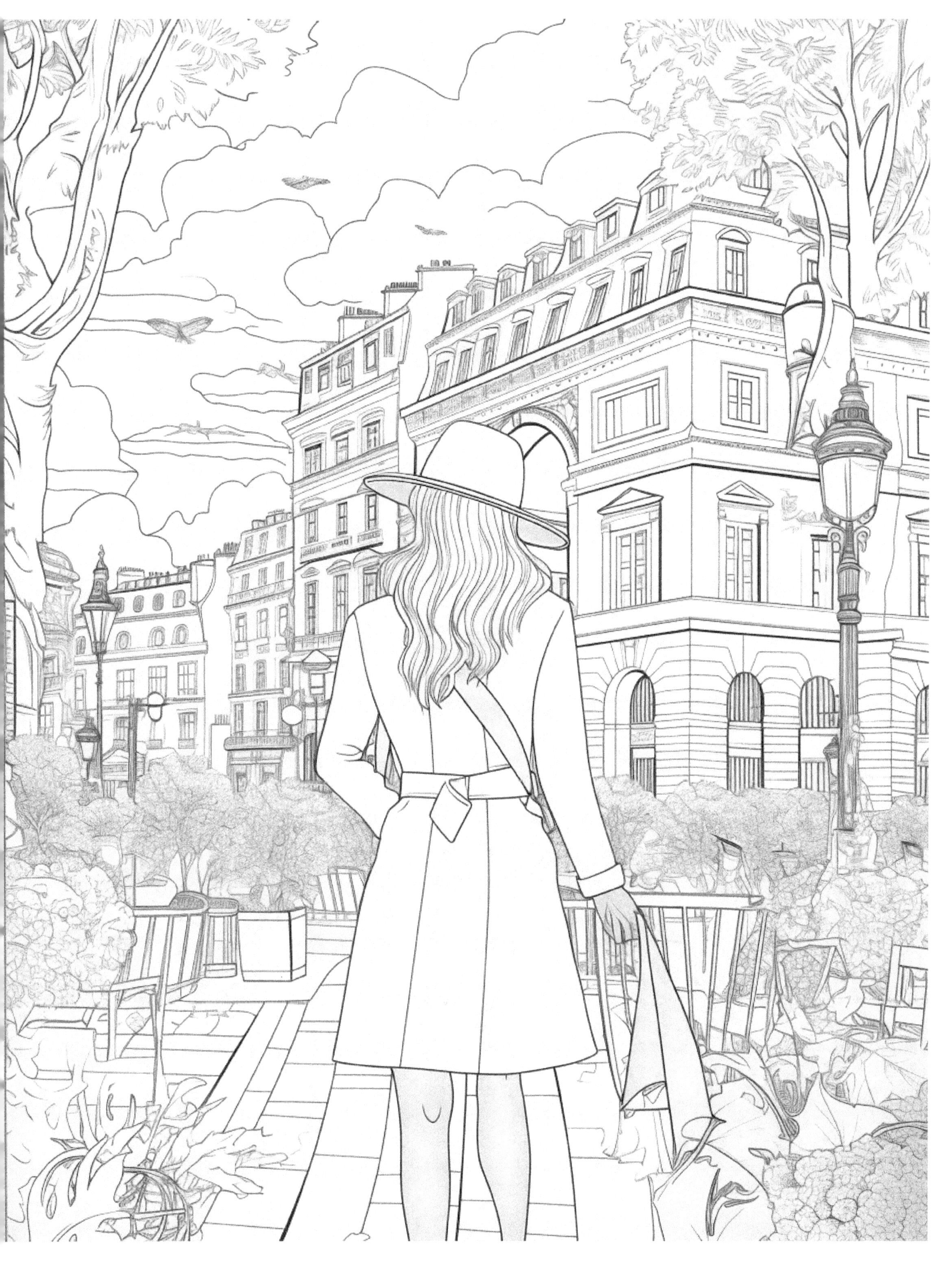

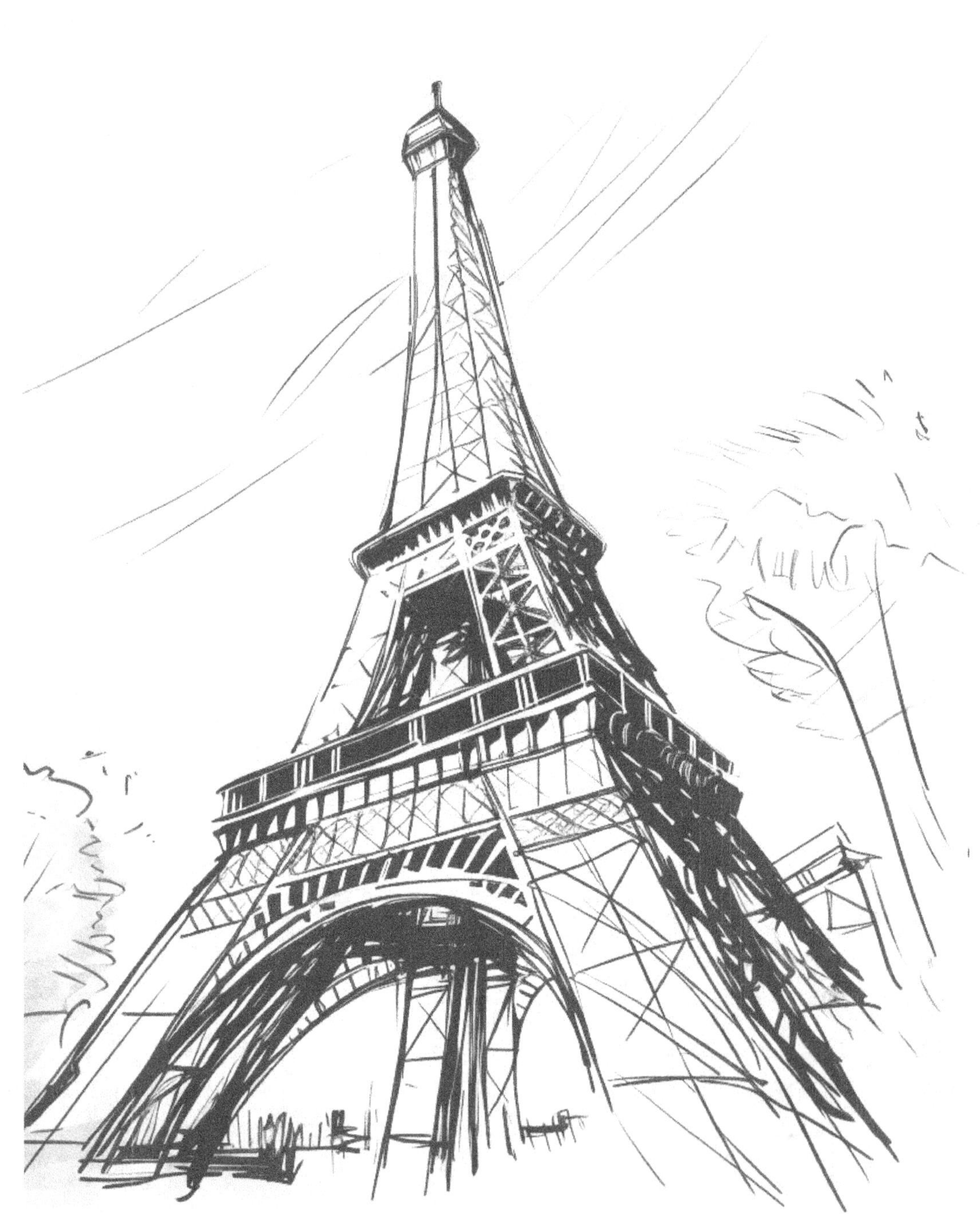

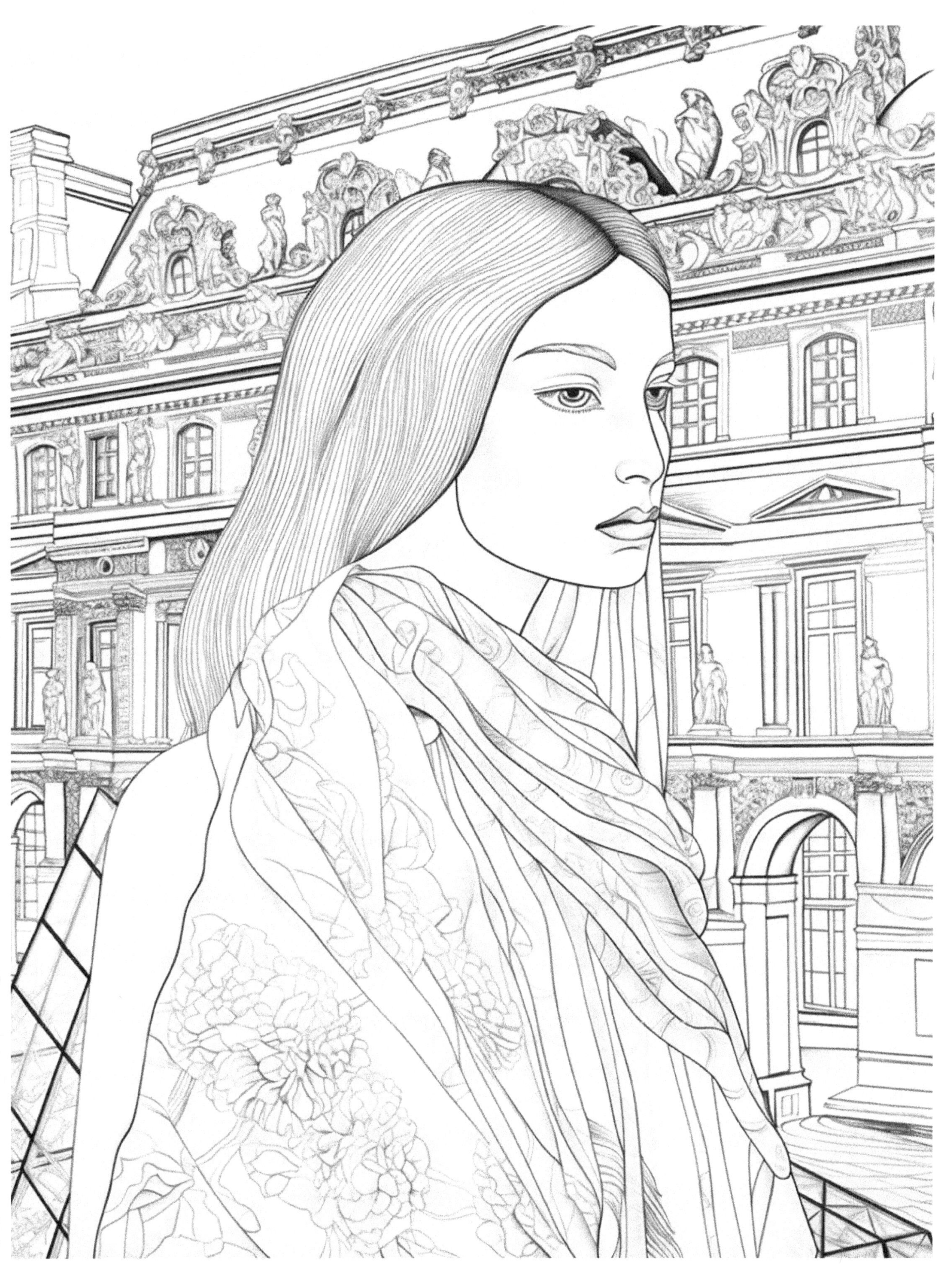

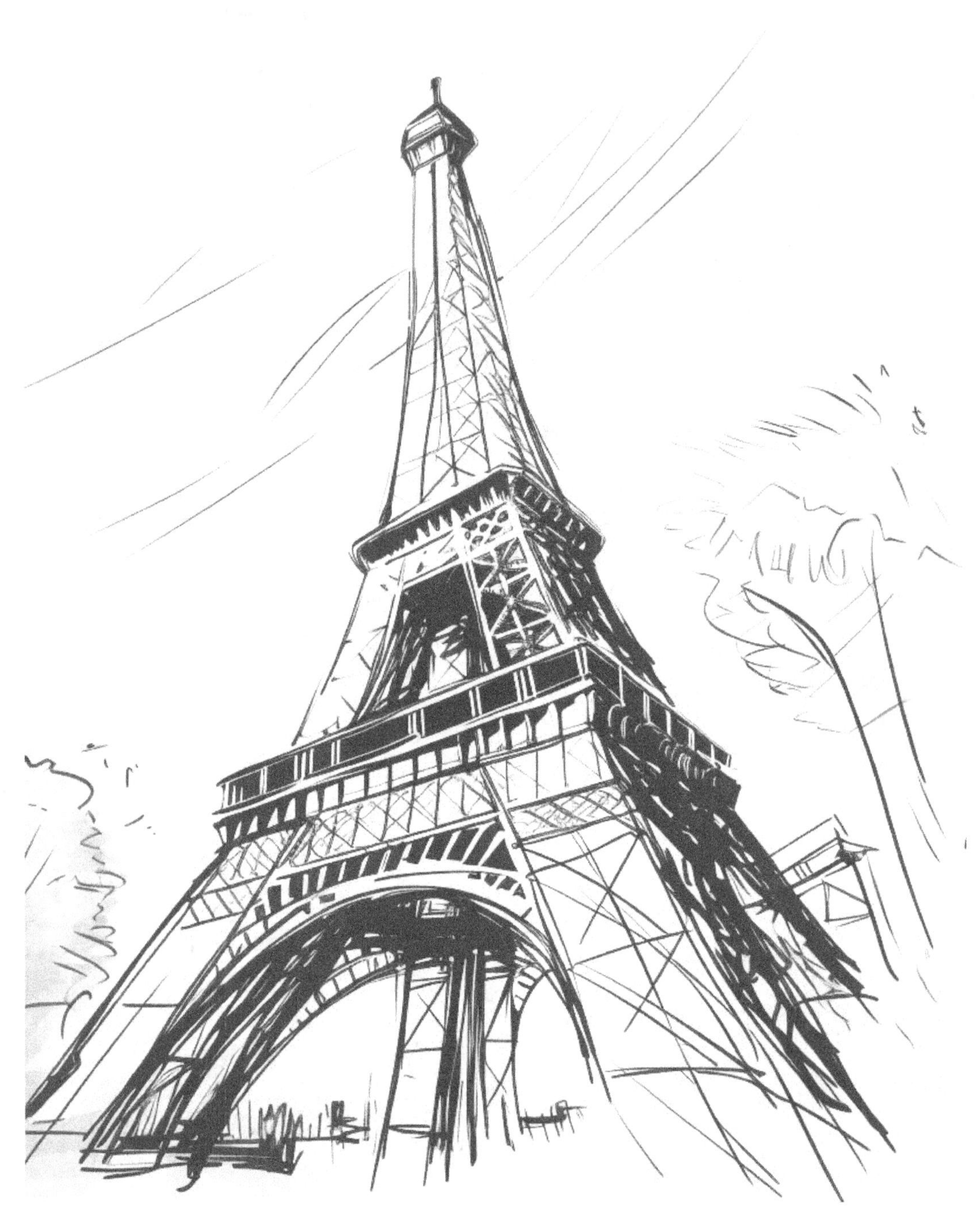

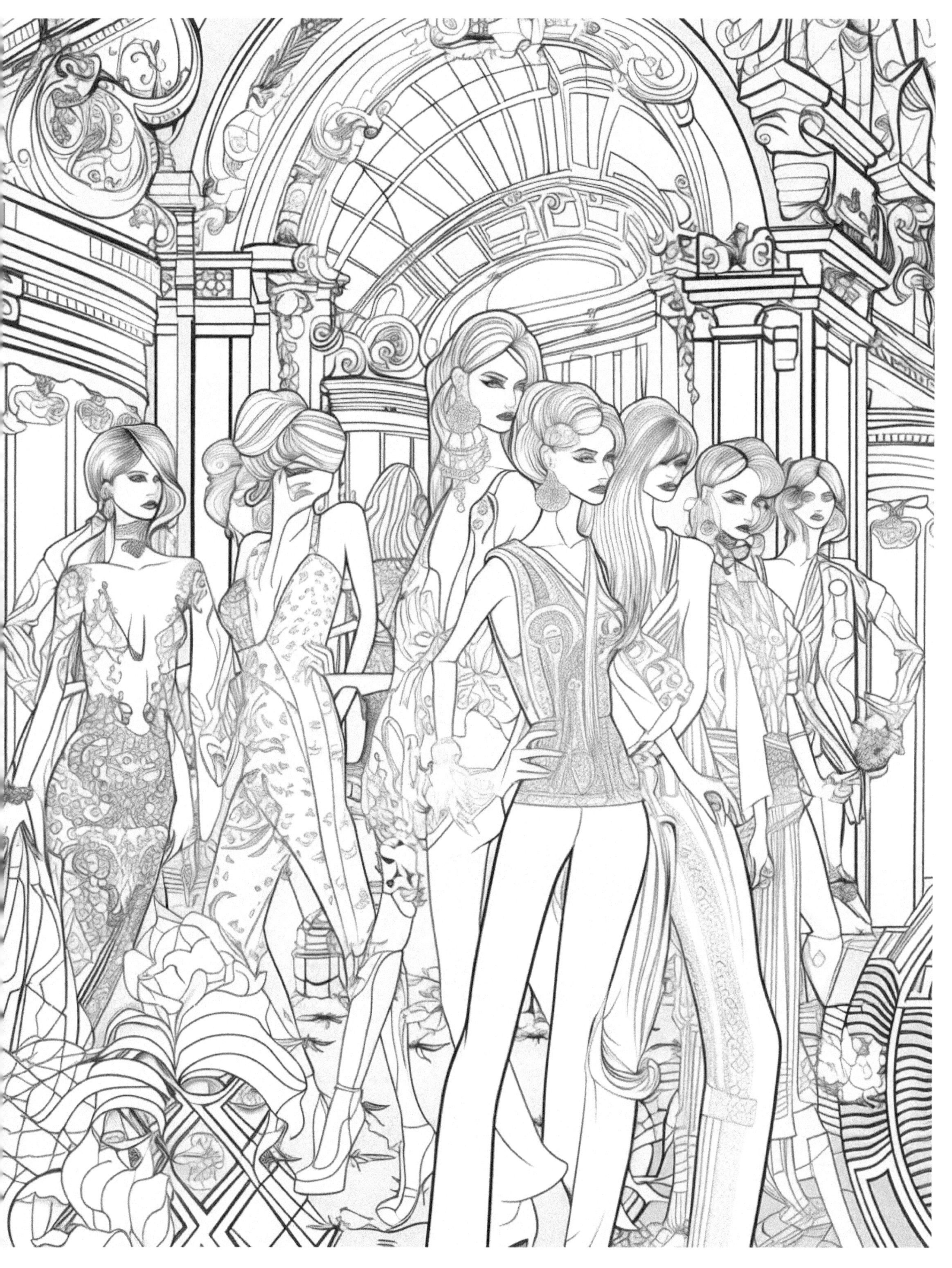

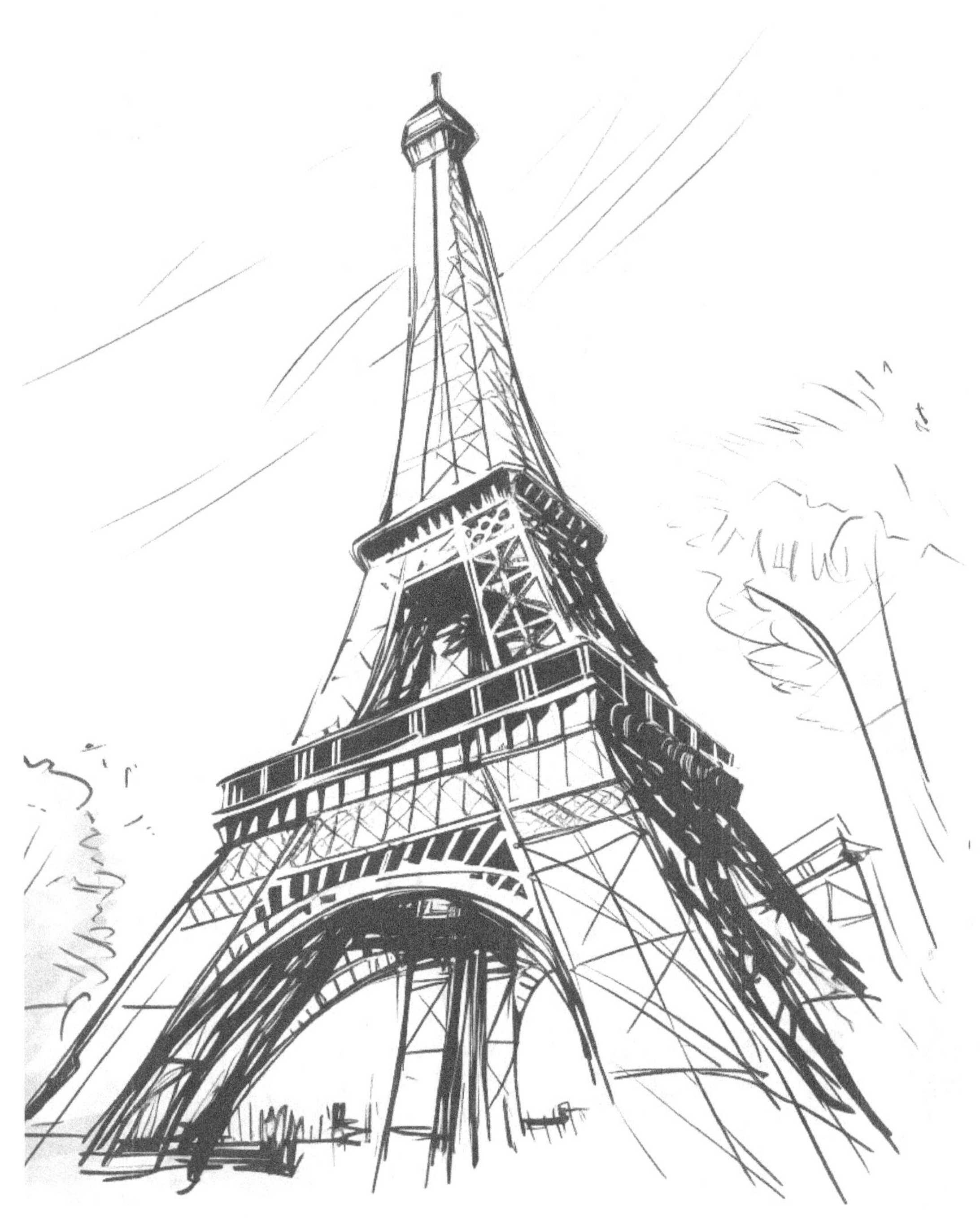

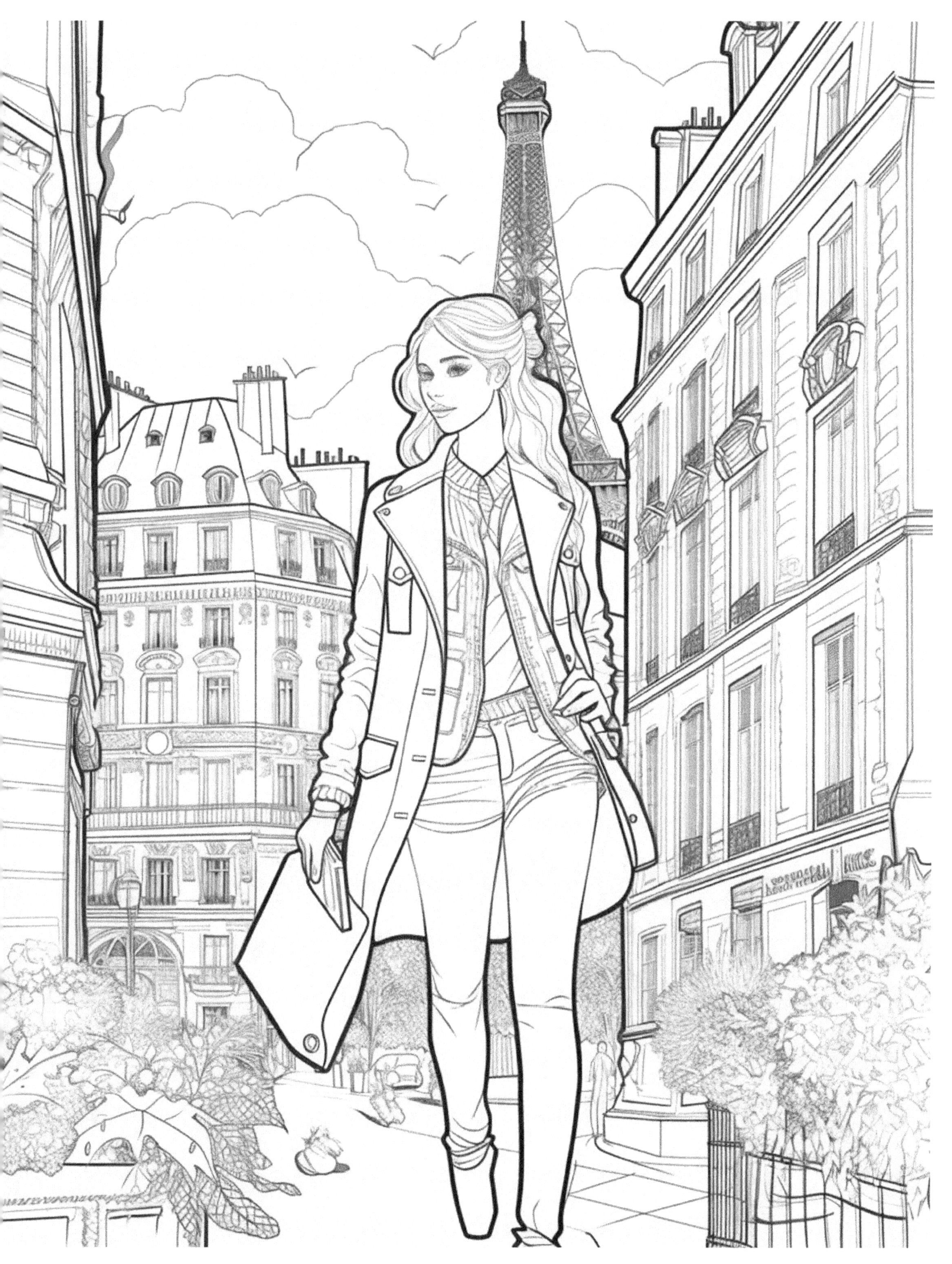

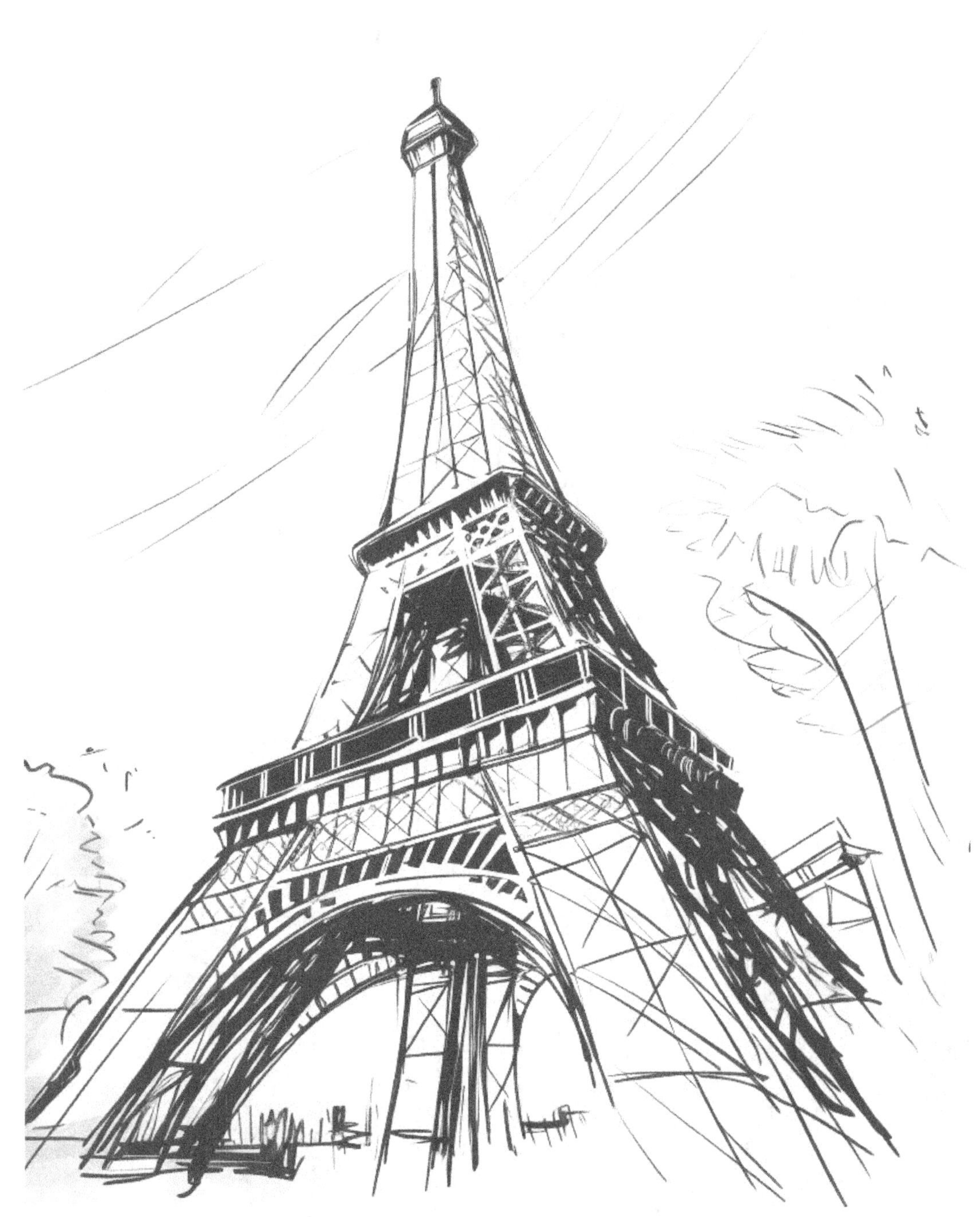

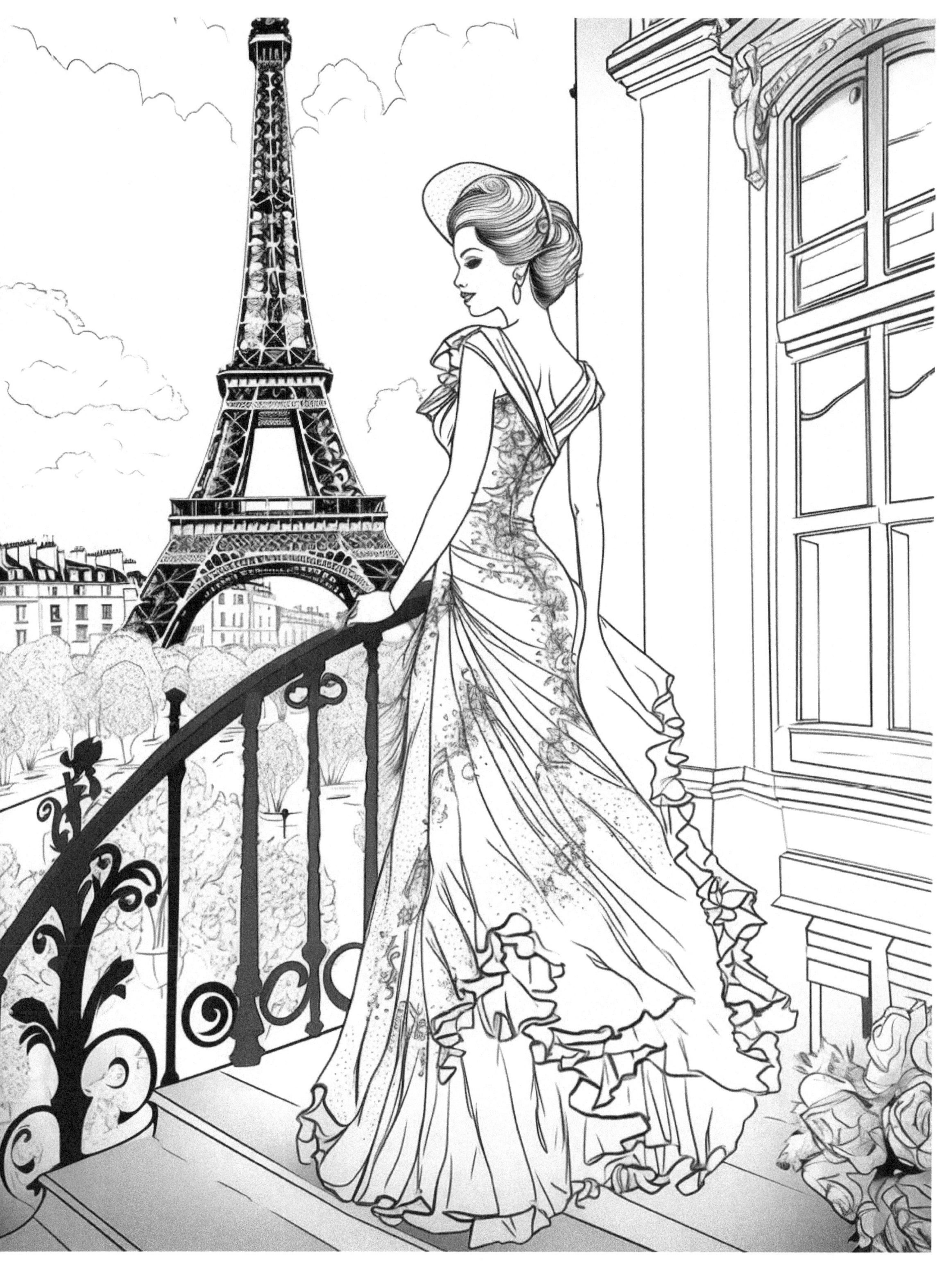

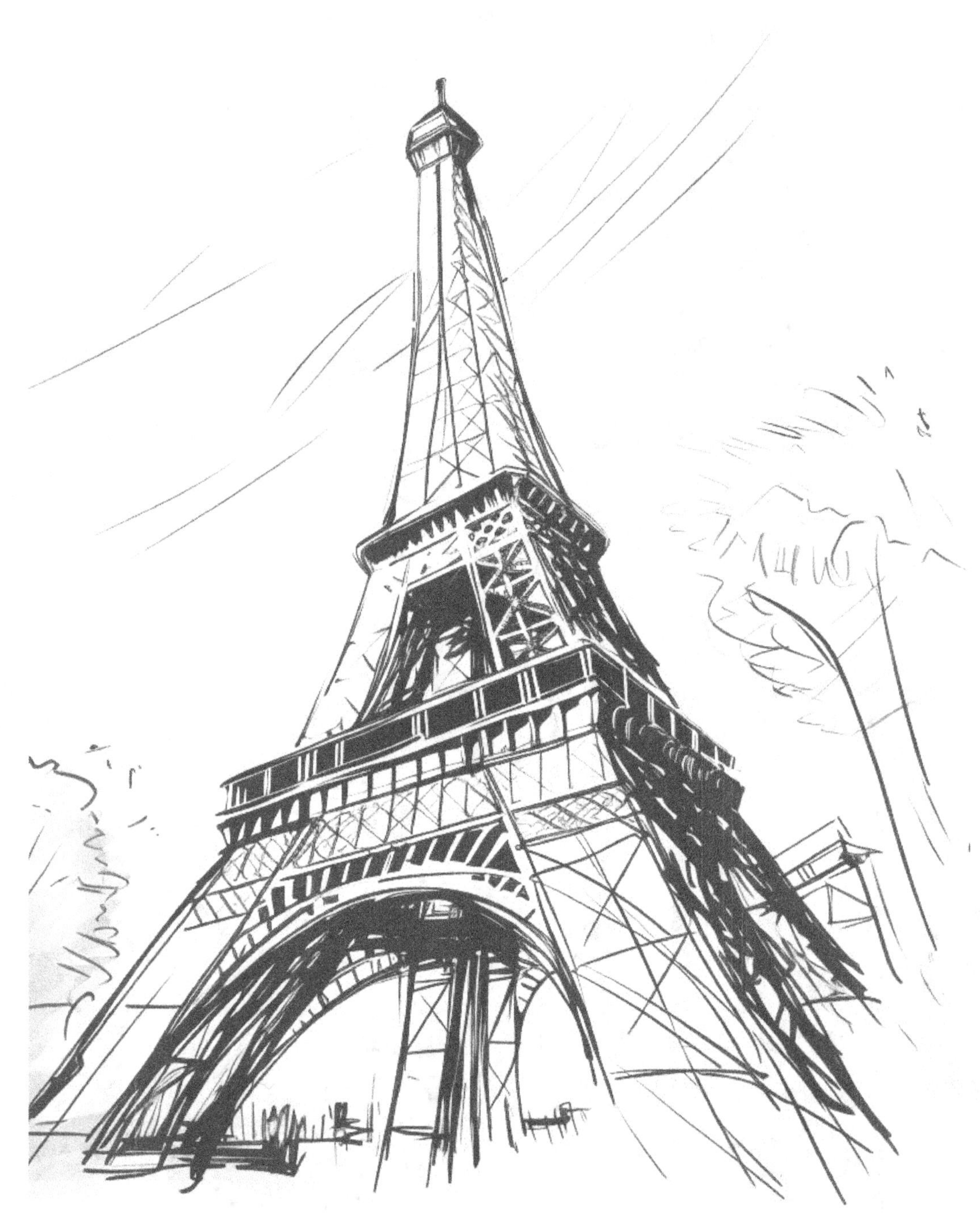

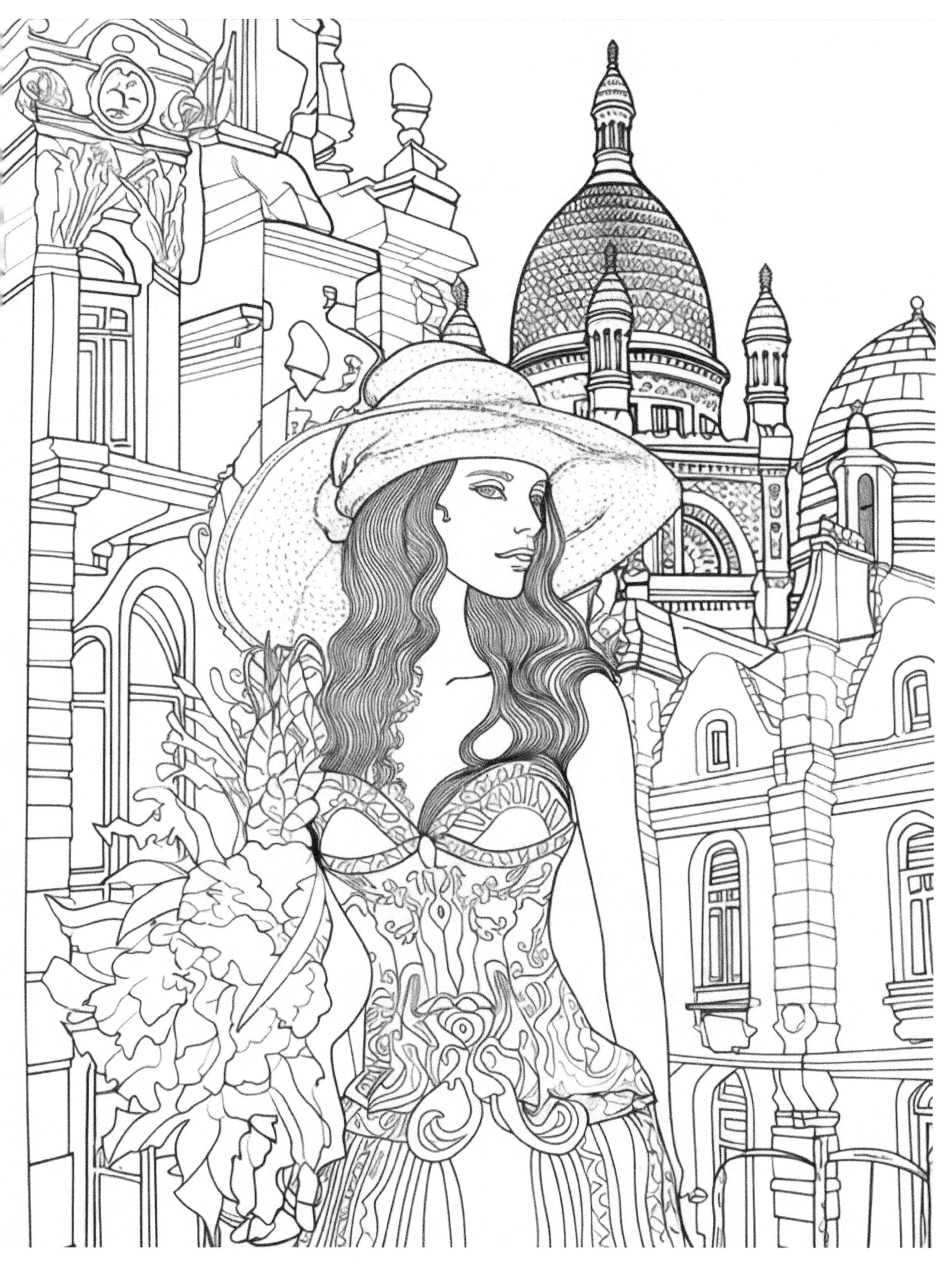

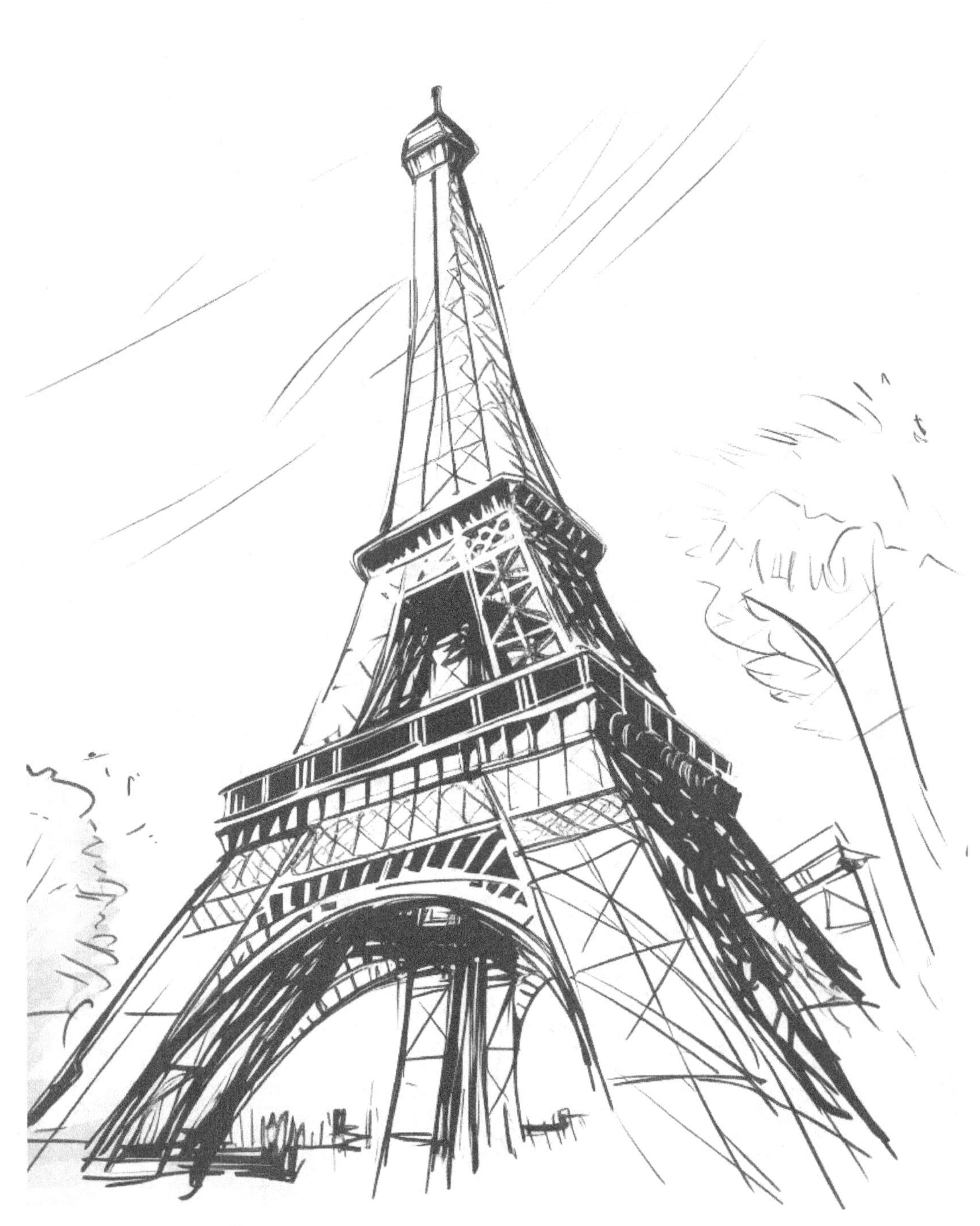

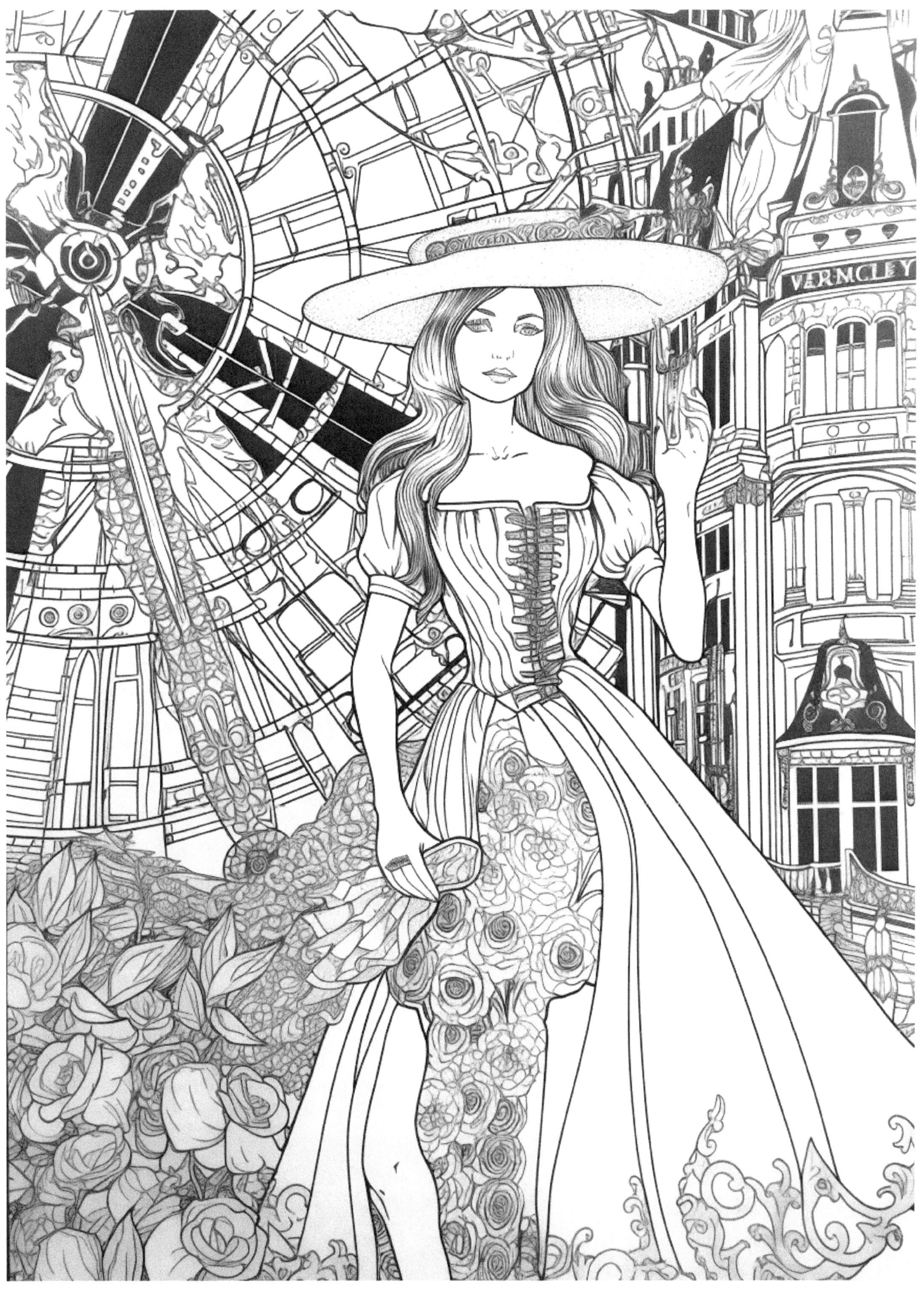
VERMCLEY